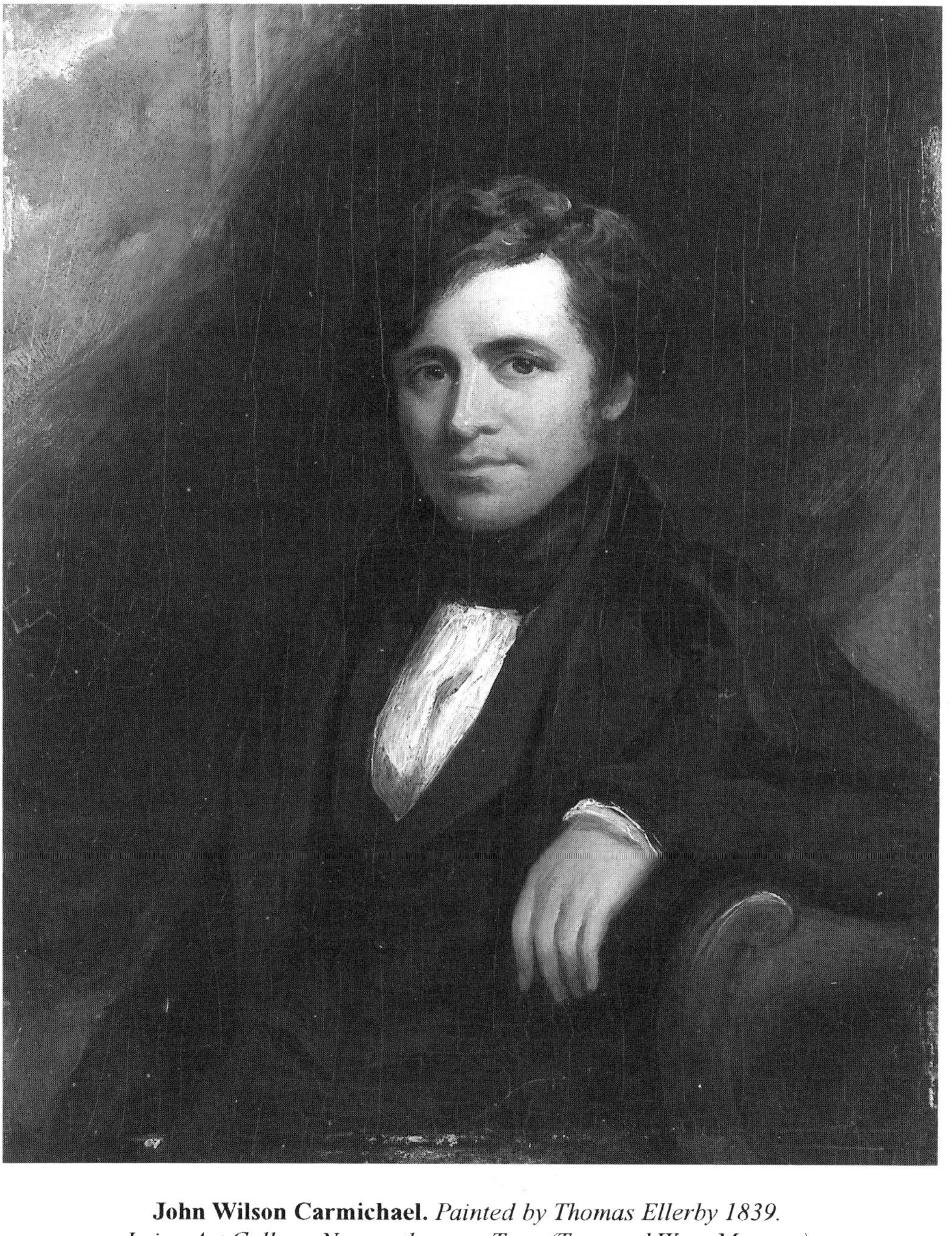

John Wilson Carmichael. *Painted by Thomas Ellerby 1839.*
Laing Art Gallery, Newcastle upon Tyne (Tyne and Wear Museum)

JOHN WILSON CARMICHAEL
1799 - 1868

by

Diana Villar

C&S

To Roger

Jacket: Part of *Newcastle from St. Ann's* (see colour plates)

First published in 1995 by Carmichael and Sweet Limited,
Professional Publishing, 48 Penny Street, Portsmouth,
Hampshire PO1 2NL, England

ISBN 1 898644 05 5

Printed and bound in Great Britain by
Biddles Ltd, Guildford and King's Lynn

CONTENTS

Note:- Wherever the word Newcastle appears, please read this as Newcastle upon Tyne.

LIST OF BLACK AND WHITE PLATES

FOREWORD

Ten years ago I found some old family papers, sketches and a private journal belonging to my great great Grandfather, John Wilson Carmichael. They were intensely revealing segments of the life of a man and an artist, albeit much further research was needed to fill in the gaps.

I was encouraged to write this by David Cordingly, who was then at the National Maritime Museum, but such a story could not have been written without help and this I have received from both official bodies and private individuals.

I am particularly grateful to Andrew Greg, Curator of the Shipley Art Gallery, Gateshead who unbeknown to me was researching Carmichael earlier as was Marshall Hall of Newcastle upon Tyne. I have also received help from Mel Twelves, Principal Commercial Officer for Tyne and Wear; the National Maritime Museum in London; the Royal Naval Museum in Portsmouth; the Bowes Museum in County Durham; the York City Art Gallery; and the Print Room in the Royal Library at Windsor Castle. The Gomshall Gallery near Guildford together with Christies, Sotheby's, Anderson and Garland, the Dean Gallery, the Omell Gallery and the Polak Gallery have amongst others willingly loaned me their photographs.

Researching someone's life would be impossible without the Records Offices and County Archivists; those in Durham, Humberside and Northumberland gave their time. As did the libraries, especially the staff of Portsmouth Central Library, Newcastle upon Tyne City Library, the North Yorkshire County Library and the Illustrated London News Picture Library.

For information about Carmichael's family tree I am grateful to members of the Carmichael, Crampton, Oliver, Sweet and Thomas families. To those I have mentioned and to others that space has forced me to omit – thank you.

Diana Villar
Portsmouth
February 1995

SHORT CHRONOLOGY

1799	June 9th. John Wilson Carmichael born in Newcastle, eldest child of William Carmichael, shipwright and Mary née Johnson.
1799	July 31st. Baptised at All Saints Church, Newcastle.
1810?	At sea during Napoleonic War.
1815?	Returned home to Newcastle. Apprenticed as a shipwright to Richard Farrington & Brothers, shipbuilders on the Tyne.
1824-25	Took up art as a career.
1826	Married Mary Sweet at Ryton Holy Cross church.
1827	Joined committee of the Northumberland Institution for the Promotion of Fine Arts.
1835	First picture exhibited at the Royal Academy.
1838	First picture exhibited at the Society of British Artists.
1846	First picture exhibited at the British Institution.
1846	Moved to London.
1847	Exhibited three pictures (his last) at the Society of British Artists.
1855	Sent to the Baltic as a war artist.
1859	Last exhibit at the Royal Academy.
1862	Last exhibit at the British Institution.
1863	Moved to Scarborough.
1868	2nd May. Died at home. Buried in Dean Road cemetery, Scarborough.

One

INTRODUCTION

When John Wilson Carmichael was born in 1799, Britain had just declared war on France and the threat of invasion from Napoleon was becoming very real. Newcastle upon Tyne, his birth-place, fared better than many others in the war years due to a flourishing coal industry and busy shipyards.

William Carmichael, John's father, worked as a shipwright in a secure job at a time when ships were badly needed. He and his wife Mary, daughter of James Johnson, were the second generation of Carmichaels to live in Newcastle for William's father had arrived there from Scotland in somewhat unusual circumstances. According to some family letters it is a romantic story.[1]

In 1746 at the time of the Jacobite Rebellion, shortly after the Battle of Culloden, William's father, Lord James Carmichael (the Scots Earldom of Hyndford), was attacked by one of Cumberland's troops while walking on his estate. In defending himself he killed the soldier. A price was then placed on his head and he was forced to hide, managing to escape from Scotland on a collier returning to Newcastle. Due to his attack he became ill and, when the collier arrived in port, the owner's daughter nursed him. She was very pretty, they fell in love and were married; and in due course William was born. Lord Carmichael felt it unsafe to stay in England too long and he decided to have a spell at sea; he was shipwrecked and died just before he could be rescued. His rescuers buried him on Sable Island in Nova Scotia.

The young wife he left behind was afraid that she and her son would get into trouble so she burnt the title deeds and any papers that could lead to her husband's identification. Thus the title became extinct. In 1760 when George III was proclaimed King, the Carmichael estates would have been restored had the title deeds been forthcoming and some of young William's friends tried to persuade him to put forward his claim, but he said that it was pointless without the papers to prove it. William's mother was a woman of great character and she maintained that it was up to him to make his own way in the world. Later with his work as a shipwright, a wife and, on the 9th June 1799, the birth of a son John Wilson, William was content.

The Carmichaels lived to the east of Newcastle, near Tyne Street off New Road (now City Road) and on the 31st July 1799 William and Mary took John Wilson to be baptised at All Saints church. Its pointed spire can still be seen for miles standing like a sentry near one of the bridges that cross the river. Two years later another boy James was born and, in 1804, a third son William.

For a description of the neighbourhood in which the young Carmichaels were brought up we must rely on a memoir that contains the fullest account of Carmichael's life and is the source of all succeeding biographies of the artist. It is written by Aaron Watson.[2] He says that at the turn of the 19th century Tyne Street would have had a row of identical brick houses with brown tiles and curved gables that sloped down the short cobbled street to the river. "Carmichael played amongst the very scenes" of which one day he would leave us records.

In another history of Newcastle[3] we learn that, at that time life for those like the Carmichaels who lived by the river centred round the Quayside. Many merchants had lived here and become wealthy; some had then moved further up into the town to quieter residential areas, while a few still remained in their tall Elizabethan style houses that faced the river. They stayed to enjoy the life with the shipowners, the shipwrights and the seamen; they watched the loading and unloading of the coalbarges and cargo ships; and there were the coastal and river vessels who called, especially when the Ascension Day Procession of Barges or other festivals took place.

On the Quayside itself there were the peddlers, the flower and fish sellers and the artists, who must have been of special interest to a young boy destined himself to become an artist. As far as is known the first painting that Carmichael sold in 1821 was one of the Quayside characters.

It is unfortunate that the sources of information that Aaron Watson had for his memoirs have now disappeared and we can only assume that John Carmichael would have attended a charity school (there was one for eighty boys and girls attached to All Saints Church), but in those war torn days school did not last long and he was sent off to serve his country.

According to a local historian Mackenzie,[4] writing in the 1820s, Carmichael went to sea "at an early age" and spent three years on a merchant vessel sailing between ports in Spain and Portugal. Aaron Watson writes that Carmichael in his boyhood "was for some time with a transport which was attached to the British fleet, and which was to a large extent laden with gunpowder". Another story comes from Trevor Blakemore in his book *The Art of Herbert Schmalz* where he tells of Carmichael returning from school at the age of twelve and "he was captured by a press-gang and shipped off to the Peninsular War as cabin boy. That war brought many strange and impressive ventures to the lad. On the powder-ship of the fleet ...." The Captain noticed Carmichael drawing sketches of ships in chalk on the decks, and it was fortunate that instead of ordering a punishment, he took an interest in the lad and gave him pencil and paper (rare luxuries at that time) so that he could “continue his studies”.

We do not know how long Carmichael spent at sea but the war with France continued that time until 1815 so it is probably right to assume that he stayed until the end of the hostilities.

Two

THE EARLY YEARS

APPRENTICED AS A CARPENTER

On his return home Carmichael was apprenticed as a shipwright to Richard Farrington & Brothers who sometime between 1810 and 1820 had set up as boat and shipbuilders, as well as being cabinet makers, carvers, gilders and joiners. It would appear that Carmichael was most fortunate to obtain work in this particular shipyard .

As employers, Richard Farrington and his brother Joseph were, according to Aaron Watson[1] "men of generous minds and liberal education, who afforded him what facilities were in their power to perfect his knowledge of art. Working as an ordinary carpenter for the most part, he was occasionally given a seat in the draughtsman's office and he found out in many ways that his employers were taking an interest in his career. He was careful nevertheless, to make himself a good workman." Watson goes on to relate a story of how devoted Carmichael was to his work that it nearly cost him his life, for one day while sketching he fell in the river and "was fished out as much dead as alive".

It was obviously a help to Carmichael that both Richard and Joseph Farrington were themselves amateur artists and (according to Mackenzie[2]) it was the latter who gave him his first box of water-colour paints. Both brothers were also friends of a Mr. Richardson and they would surely have mentioned to him their employee's talent for drawing.

Thomas Miles Richardson was born in Newcastle in 1784 and as a young man had been trained as a cabinet maker, then a schoolmaster, but in his spare time he taught himself to paint and soon decided to make art his career. He became well known in the north of England for his Northumberland scenery and his views of the Lake District and Scotland and when, in 1814, he exhibited at the Royal Academy a painting of the *Old Fish Market in Newcastle,* he became a national figure. Paul Usherwood in his *Art for Newcastle* says that "Richardson established himself as a busy topographical illustrator, landscape and marine painter, in a town which at the time had virtually no artistic – no painting tradition".

We know that Carmichael became the friend and probably a pupil of Richardson's and we know that Richardson taught "more or less every day of his life". But we also know that in 1821 it was Joseph Farrington who obtained

Carmichael a commission to paint a picture for the Corporation of Trinity House, Newcastle upon Tyne. This still hangs there today – it is neither a marine nor a landscape painting, but a character entitled *Blind Willie*.

For as long as anyone could remember this unfortunate person had been seen around the Quayside and the various markets, circulating with thieves and vagabonds, and his reputation was no better than theirs. His full misshapen face with its sightless eyes was perhaps good practice for a young artist who was never going to be happy painting close-ups of people. With *Blind Willie* Carmichael also chose a popular if unattractive figure who was well known to everyone for his unmelodious voice singing simple songs accompanied by his violin. The artist wrote at the bottom "Drawn by John Wilson Carmichael. 28th July 1821". This is probably the first dated picture we have. All his future work would be signed J.W. Carmichael or initialled, J.W.C.

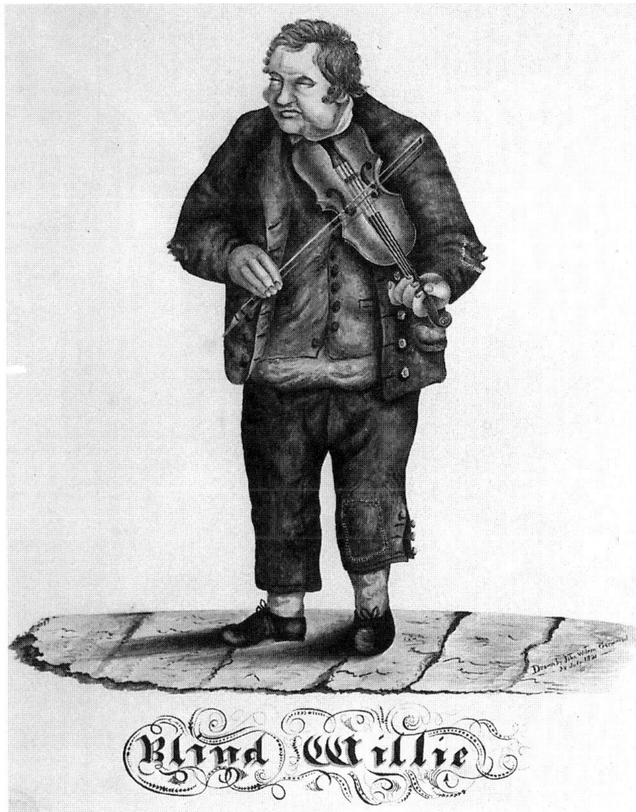

Blind Willie.
Corporation of the Newcastle upon Tyne Trinity House

NORTHUMBERLAND INSTITUTION FOR THE PROMOTION OF FINE ARTS

It was a year later in 1822 that Richardson together with a local friend Henry Perlee Parker[3] decided to set about changing the artistic scene in Newcastle in the hope of encouraging artists to stay and work in the north east. One of the ways the two men decided to do this was to form a committee of local artists who would hold an annual art exhibition in the town, they would also hold loan exhibitions of old Masters and encourage well-known artists from around the country to show and sell their work. Middlebrook[4] in his book *Newcastle upon Tyne* quotes Richard Welford's blunt words when he says "In 1822 when Richardson was 38 and Parker 27, with a venturesomeness that compels admiration, the two friends formed the Northumberland Institution for the Promotion of the Fine Arts".

Edward Swinburne,[5] the landscape and figure painter, another close friend of Richardson, was asked to be President. Also on the committee were the famous artist and wood engraver Thomas Bewick[6] and Robert his son. Then there was Joseph Crawhall[7] a landscape, figure and animal painter; John Dobson[8] an architect and landscape painter, who was to become a life-long friend of Carmichael; and the final member of the committee was James Ramsay[9], a portrait, historical and landscape painter who was already a well-known exhibitor in London before he arrived in Newcastle.

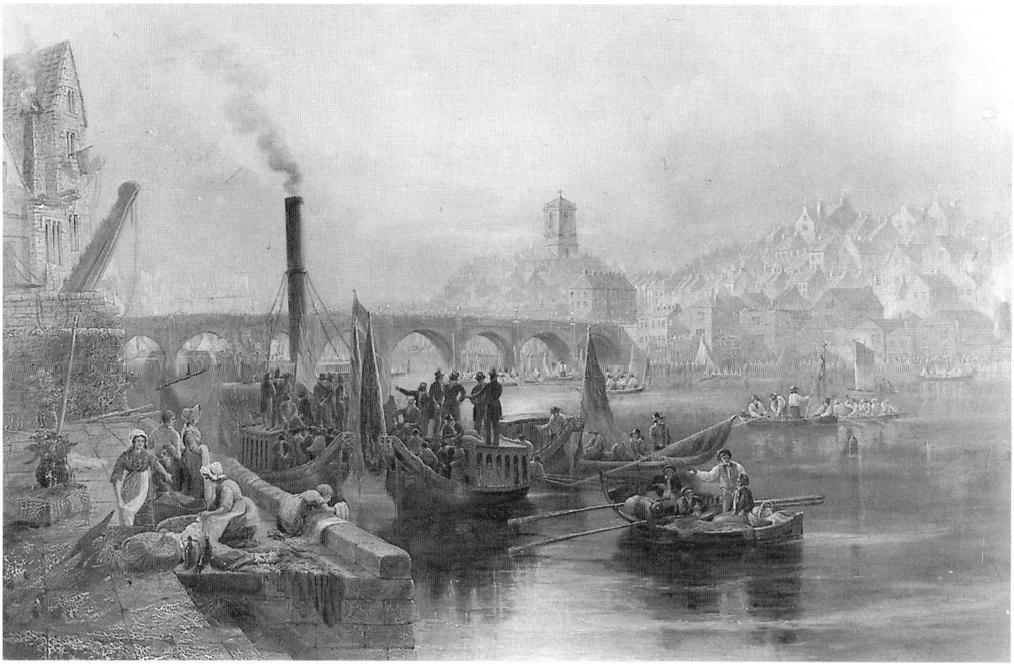

Barge Day-Morning. *Bowes Museum, Co. Durham*
Carmichael painted this in 1829 and received favourable comments in the local newspaper. "A very creditable picture of this promising artist". Carmichael may have been influenced by a similar one painted by Thomas Richardson six years previously.

The first exhibition was held in Richardson's own house at 4 Brunswick Place; it opened on 23rd September and closed on 16th November. It is impossible to say how many people would have paid their shilling entrance fee or bought a season ticket for 5/- and an extra 6d for a catalogue, but the exhibition was an instant success. Carmichael would have certainly been there, for ever since he had painted his Trinity House picture he really could think of himself as an artist. But who were the other artists around at this time?

CONTEMPORARY ARTISTS

In Newcastle itself there was John Wykeham Archer,[10] a painter in watercolour but who was to become known for his engravings. Robert Mackreth,[11] the landscape and coastal marine painter had arrived in Newcastle from London and he exhibited at that first exhibition. George Gibsone[12] showed his plant paintings and Thomas Good[13] his portraits, landscapes and coastal scenes. There was John Martin,[14] the historical, biblical and landscape painter whose family had moved to Newcastle partly because he wanted to paint.

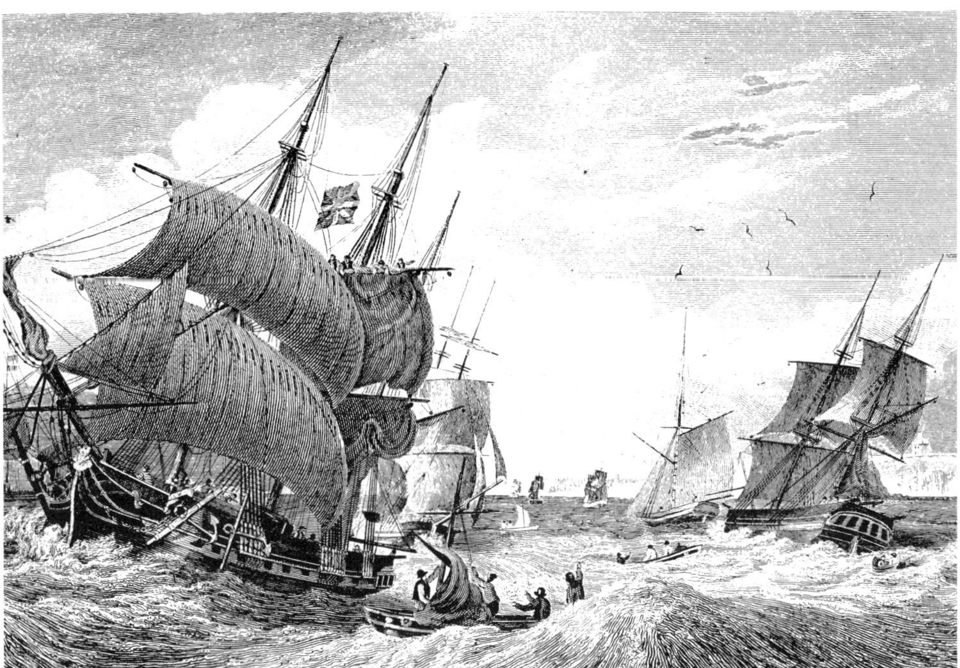

Tynemouth Bar. *Hindson Print. Photographer Robin Crampton*
One of Carmichael's earlier dramatic seascapes

Amongst those who were to eventually develop into mainly marine artists was George Balmer[15] who came to Newcastle from a house decorating business in Edinburgh. He became a great personal friend of Carmichael and for the rest of their lives the two had a light hearted rivalry. Also from Edinburgh came John Ewbank,[16] a landscape, coastal and marine artist who exhibited at that first exhibition. Like Balmer, Ewbank had started his working life as a house painter until, as with Carmichael, a kindly employer had noticed his talent for art and encouraged him to pursue it as a career. In those days a number of the younger artists were also concentrating on painting landscapes, not just in Newcastle but nationally, for ever since the late 17th century rich landowners had wanted their houses and estates painted; so landscapes had become the artist's bread and butter.

The exhibitions at the Northumberland Institution also gave the local artists a chance to see the work of nationally known painters, and names such as Landseer,[17] Haydon,[18] Varley[19] and J.F. Lewis[20] the figure-painter appear. There were paintings from A. Callcott,[21] George Chambers,[22] Clarkson Stanfield[23] and Francis Danby[24] from London; J,B. Chrome[25] – the son of old Chrome of the Norwich school and John Ward[26] from the Hull school sent their work; David Cox[27] the eminent watercolourist, exhibited at the Northumberland Institution; and J.T. Serres,[28] Marine painter to the King, exhibited there before he died.

In the eyes of the art reviewers of the 1820s and 1830s, the success of the Newcastle exhibitions depended not on the local exhibitors but on the national ones. Artists, especially from London, had to be persuaded to send their work so that potential buyers would come to Newcastle, for the town did not have a name for good selling prices. Only two exhibition catalogues include price lists and they suggest that the average Newcastle price for a cabinet-size oil painting was £25 and for a normal size watercolour, just over £6. Higher sums would be asked for larger and more ambitious works, and important pictures from London celebrities could go for much more. There is one account of Danby asking £200 for one of his paintings; in Newcastle it seemed a lot of money but not so by London standards.

MOVE TO OWN STUDIO

No doubt there would have been a lot of excitement amongst the less well known marine artists when Joseph Mallard Turner[29] sent any of his work, even though the reviewer in the Newcastle Courant for 21st June 1828 appeared to have had some trouble in understanding Turner's two exhibits for that year, *Briebrich Palace* and *Marksburg,*[30] when he said "I question that even the name of Turner will procure admirers for these pictures. Indeed without his name they would not be noted at all .....".

However these views were perhaps not shared by the younger artists who mostly admired his work and Carmichael was no exception – but this will be discussed later in greater depth. During those first exhibitions in the 1820s Carmichael was basically an onlooker. We know he was still apprenticed to Farrington in 1824 because he wrote on a picture that was in the Thomas Sopwith collection – "drawn before I left my business as a Carpenter. 1824"[31] so it was probably not until the following year that, encouraged by his friends, he left the shipyard. He established himself in his own studio in what is now City Road, a short walk from where he had been born and had worked in Farrington's shipyard.

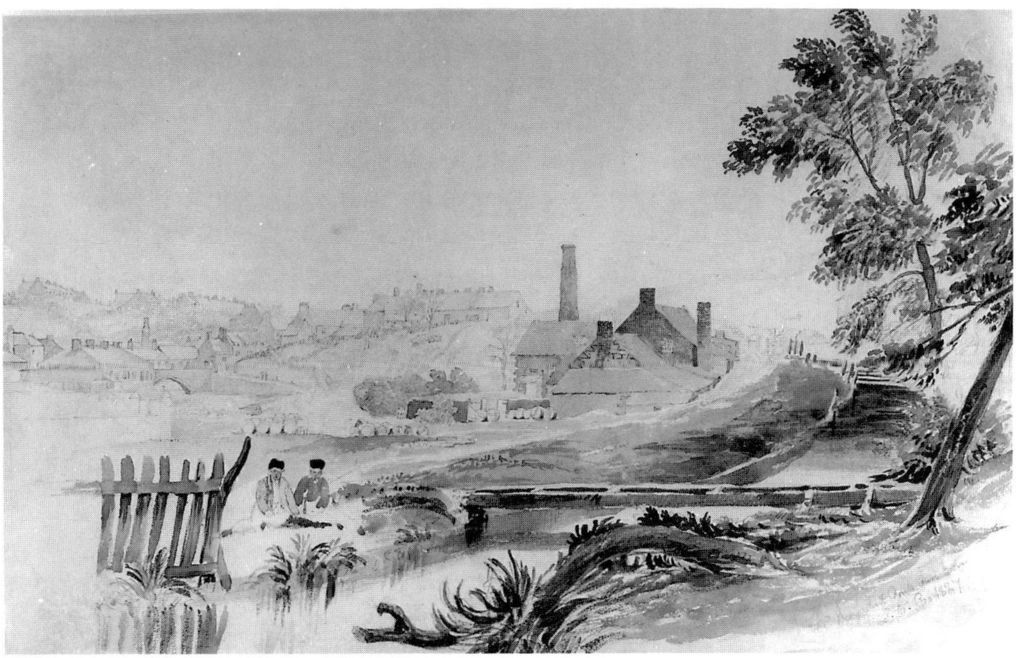

Mr Reay's Flint Mill, Ouseburn. *Laing Art Gallery. Newcastle upon Tyne*
Painted in 1827. This is the earliest dated Carmichael drawing in the Laing Art Gallery.

Three

ART AS A CAREER

COST OF PAINTING MATERIALS

Carmichael was now dependent on his art for his living and inevitably those first months would have contained the familiar pressures experienced by all the self-employed – in order to live and to buy the materials he required, he must sell his work.

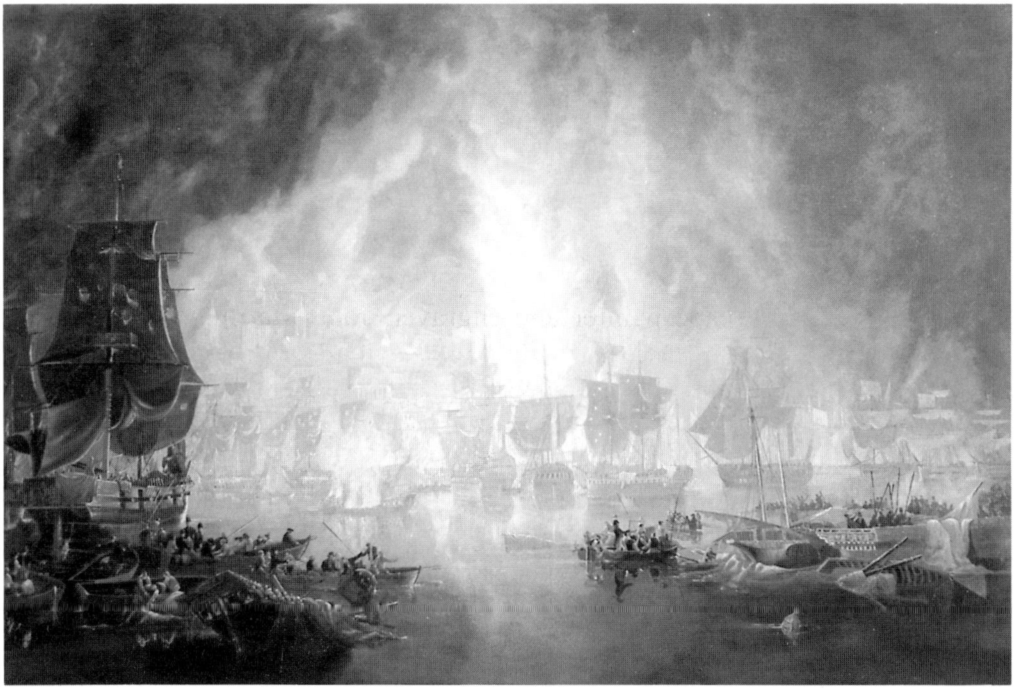

The Bombardment of Algiers.
The Corporation of the Newcastle upon Tyne Trinity House . Photographer A.L.C. Wilkinson

In those days you could pay anything from 2d to 5d for a good drawing pencil; a ten inch oval palette cost 1/-; and large sable paint brushes in quills could cost as much as 10/- each. Many different types of brushes and paints would be needed for a picture and that was without the paper or canvas. The smallest drawing board would have cost at least 1/3d – that is if it was made of mahogany. And a 10" x 7" sketch book of thick paper was 5/-. When you compare these prices with the 13 guineas that John Carmichael received for his first major historical work and consider the time such a work would have taken, there would have been little money to spare.

FIRST TWO HISTORICAL PICTURES

Sea battles make excellent subjects for those artists able to paint them and for one of his first Carmichael chose *The Fight between The Shannon and The Chesapeake* which had taken place in 1812 between the British and the Americans. The *Shannon* was probably Britain's most efficient ship afloat in those days and the action against the *Chesapeake* only lasted about a quarter of an hour. But by the time the British had boarded and captured her, the Americans had lost about a third of their crew. It was a fierce bloody fight and Carmichael portrayed it well, as he did his second historical piece which was another commission from Trinity House – *The Bombardment of Algiers – 1816*. This picture, for which he received 40 guineas, is still on the walls of the Newcastle upon Tyne Trinity House. In this large oil, while appropriate for the subject, Carmichael has used rather uncharacteristic yellows and blacks more in the style of another local landscape painter and engraver, John Martin.[1] While Martin was 10 years his senior, the two artists were friends and in 1821 Martin's *Belshazzar's Feast* had won acclaim in London and elsewhere.

Whether or not Carmichael had Martin's dramatic painting of *Belshazzar's Feast* in mind when he painted his *Bombardment of Algiers*, the result is a great picture which, since it was begun some years after the battle, must have required much research to ensure the correct ships were at the scene and the sky right for the time of day. Carmichael well deserved the praise he received not just for his obvious attention to detail but for his rapid mastery in the medium of oil painting. By 1827, when he had probably only been painting in oils for at the most five years, he painted *The Wreck of the Betsy Cains* (also known as *Tynemouth Cliffs*) which, especially in its composition, is considered by many to be one of his greatest oil paintings (see colour plates).

Like many artists Carmichael took pupils and we know of two. One was John Scott[2] who was slightly younger than his master and shared the same interests in marine subjects. Scott was also skilled in making models of ships, yachts and other vessels so perhaps the master could also learn from his pupil. Another was Thomas Thorpe,[3] a lithographer and landscape painter in both oil and watercolour who was one of Carmichael's most gifted pupils.

So by 1826 life was going well for John Carmichael and to complete it, Mary Sweet entered his life. Mary came from a family of five; her father was a Freeman of the City and they lived in New Road near where Carmichael had his studio. He and Mary married on March 20th 1826 in Ryton, a small village outside Newcastle at the Church of the Holy Cross. That part of the Parish Register 'with consent of' is left blank and the witnesses at the ceremony were John Penmara and Henry Dorn who were not members of either the Carmichael or Sweet families. As they and the curate George Watson have long since gone, we will probably never know for certain if the families were represented.

This drawing of Ryton looking towards the east is one that Carmichael probably did about this time; the only building shown is the spire of the church and he has drawn attention to this with a swirl of cloud. This was used later as an engraving in a series entitled *Views on the Tyne.*

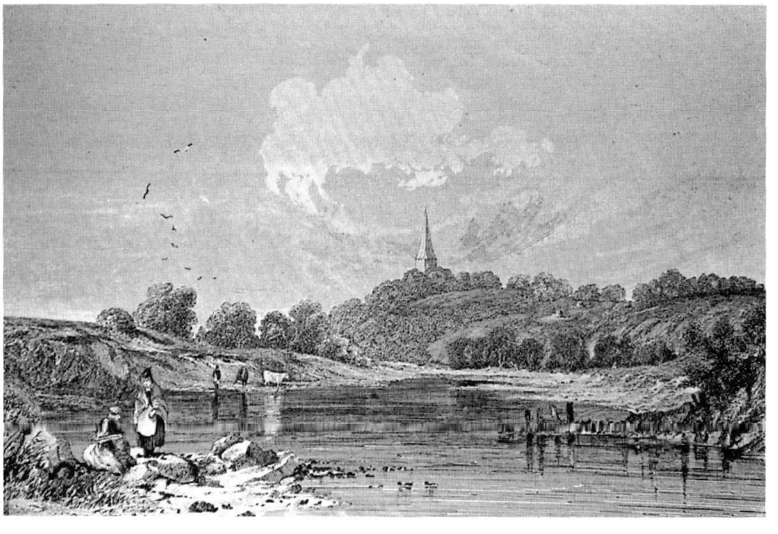

Ryton Church.
Hindson Print.
Photographer
Robin Crampton

The young Carmichael's first child, a daughter, was born the following December and they called her Margaret and added a second name Bell which was Mary's mother's maiden name. Just before Christmas the baby was baptised at All Saints church and in the register under 'Occupation of Father', Carmichael wrote "Drawing Master". It was twenty seven years since he himself had been baptised in the same church.

In a local Directory for 1833 Carmichael is mentioned as being a landscape and marine painter and teacher of drawing, and some biographies mention that he gave lessons in miniature painting. Marshall Hall, author of *Artists of Northumbria* says that this could have come from a trade directory of the day. With hindsight it is strange that Carmichael should offer this service for he was never too happy painting faces and the two copies he made of miniatures that Thomas Carrick did of himself and Mary are not good though they give some idea of what they both looked like soon after their marriage.

It shows Carmichael with an oval shaped, sensitive face. He has a generous mouth and high cheek bones that were clean shaven in those days; his hair is dark brown and curly and a few loose curls are falling onto his high forehead. His eyes are hazel and there is a look of determination in them together with a sense of fun. On the other hand Mary's blue eyes look sad; her face is slightly rounder than that of her husband; her features are more pointed; and her mouth is small. Her hair is auburn and curls fall to her shoulders. She looks a little shy; perhaps she was the right partner for someone who was ambitious and at times an extrovert.

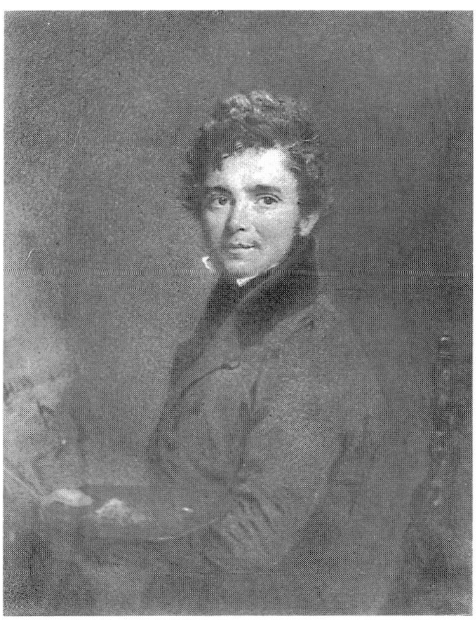

John Wilson Carmichael.
Private Collection
Photographer Robin Crampton

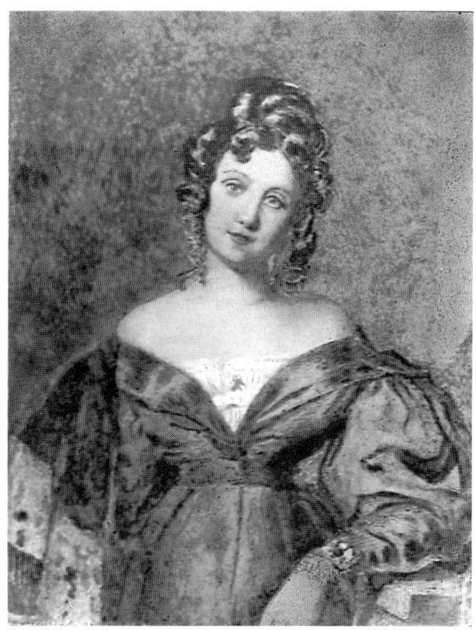

Mary Sweet.
Private Collection
Photographer Robin Crampton

OTHER ASPECTS OF ART

At this point it is interesting to note that as early as 1827 the historian E. Mackenzie[4] was writing of Carmichael, "It may be confidently predicted that the industry, genius and enthusiasm of this artist will ultimately raise him to a very high rank in the profession he has chosen".

Apart from his drawing and painting Carmichael developed an interest in architecture. This may have been due to his friendship with John Dobson,[5] an architect who was on the committee of the Northumberland Institution, and was active with the city planners who were demolishing, designing and building in Newcastle in the 1820s. Dobson, while being himself an architectural and landscape painter needed someone to colour his drawings, and to add the figures and bring his designs to life; so he and Carmichael collaborated and this developed into a life-long friendship. As late as 1855 when Carmichael was in Hamburg he was thinking of Dobson when he wrote on 28th May: "The old part of the town is very rich in ornaments of all ages, some of the doorways are perfectly beautiful. I regretted having no time or I would have sketched some of them for my kind friend Mr. Dobson. Some of the gable ends would have made his mouth water, much more elaborate than the fronts of the old Presses which we used to look at together".[6]

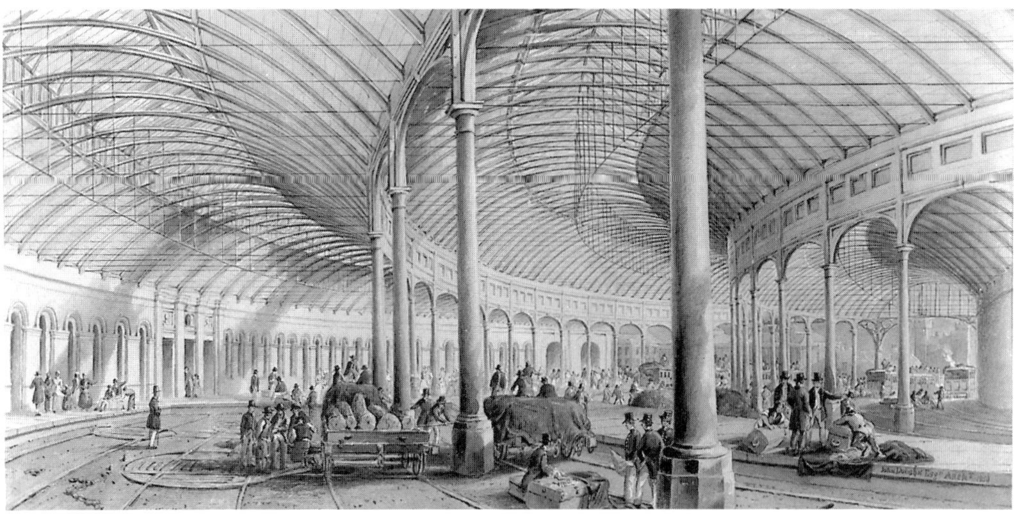

The Interior of Central Station, Newcastle upon Tyne.
Laing Art Gallery, Newcastle upon Tyne (Tyne and Wear Museum)
Carmichael's initials are on the trunk and Dobson's name to the right.

John Dobson and Carmichael worked together on several architectural designs. One was Beaufront Castle near Hexham that Dobson rebuilt; another was Brinkburn Grange. In this case both artists were helping each other for they were in preparation for two oils that Carmichael did of the former in 1845. Another two designs they both worked on were *The Interior of Grainger Market* and *The Interior of Central Station, Newcastle upon Tyne*. Here Carmichael has inscribed at the bottom with his signature "sketched on the spot".

But whenever he could Carmichael went back to the sea for his pictures and in 1825 he exhibited for the first time, at the Northumberland Institution, two seascapes – *Outward and homeward bound Indiamen passing the Downs* and *A Seventy-four in a heavy sea.*

Over the next two years the Institution, that had started so well, began to be criticised by the press who said that it was nothing more than a private speculation on the part of Thomas Miles Richardson. Exhibitors began to decline and 1827 was the last year of the Institution's existence. The committee, who that year were joined by Carmichael, decided that they had the right idea but they would start again and expand it. It would be moved from Mr. Richardson's house into a specially designed Art Gallery and would be known as the Northern Academy of Arts which brought it into line with the Academies of London and Edinburgh.

John Dobson was behind the architecture of the new building. A plot of land was bought for £113-10/- and the gallery took shape. It was an unusual classical design with two large Corinthian columns and recessed central bays on the first storey and, with its ornamental polished stone front, it contrasted with the other brick buildings in the street. But it was imposing as well as functional and the elegance of the design and decor inside more than compensated for the outside.

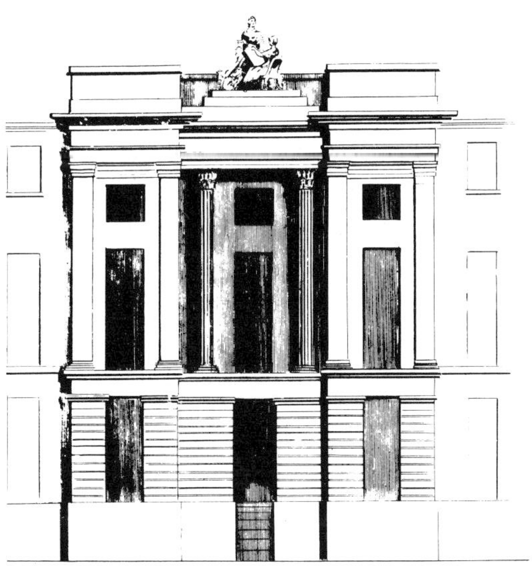

Northern Academy of Arts. c.1828.
Newcastle upon Tyne City Library

FIRST PUBLICATION

In 1832 Carmichael took his first step into publishing when together with another artist, J. Metcalfe, he did eight views of Fountains Abbey that were later engraved and which the printers, Blackwell & Co. of Newcastle advertised as being "intended to illustrate the Architecture and Picturesque Scenery of that Celebrated Ruin".[7]

Around this time the Carmichaels have an address in the north of Newcastle, 9 Northumberland Court, one of a cluster of fashionable courts in a narrow street. It was a pleasant residential district which earlier would have been outside the city walls. Carmichael had moved his studio next door to the new Northern Academy of Arts on the south side of Blackett Street a short walk from his home.

After the view of the river Tyne, the shipping and the atmosphere of the waterfront with its Quayside characters, it must have seemed like another world to the artist for it was to the world of rivers, sea and shipping that Carmichael would return whenever he needed the ideas or the details for some of his best pictures.

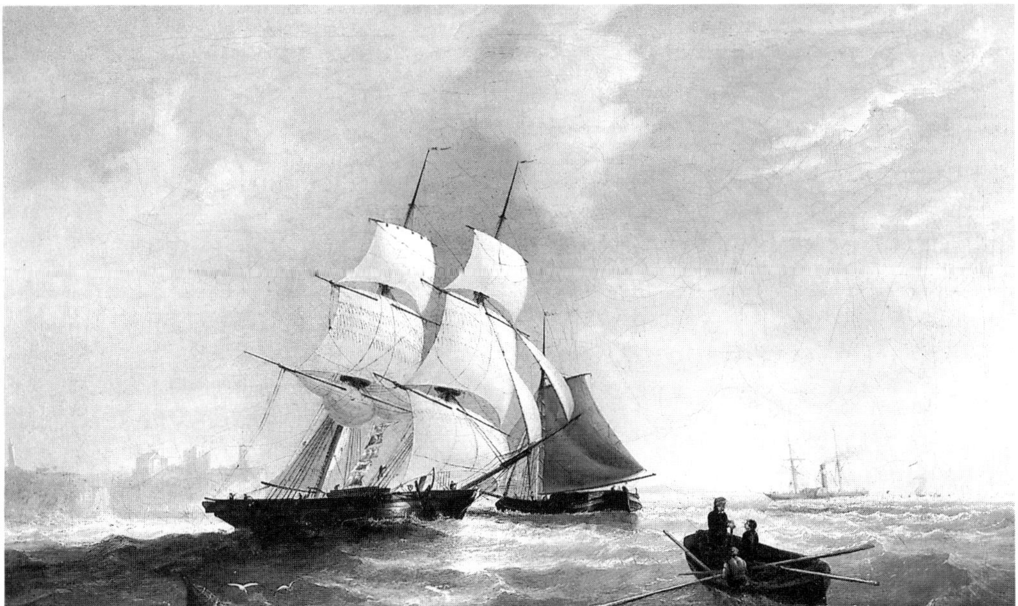

Shipping off the entrance to the Tyne. *Old Solent House Galleries, Lymington*
Carmichael enjoyed introducing different types of vessels into his compositions.

Four

CARMICHAEL'S TRAVELS

After hostilities with France ended, artists began to travel, for the Napoleonic Wars had cut England off from the art world on the Continent. So many artists wanted to see for themselves the masterpieces of other countries, especially the treasures that Napoleon had acquired for the Louvre in Paris.

Carmichael was no exception and the Laing Gallery in Newcastle hold many of his sketches done 'on the spot'. Most are dated in the 1830s and 1840s and Watson[1] in his memoir mentions Carmichael's "frequent travels". But he only refers to one actual year, 1861, when the artist "visited Calais and Dunkerque, and brought home sketches from which several pictures were painted in that and subsequent years".

We do have a number of sketches that he signed 'on the spot' from places like *Sidon*, *Castle of the Dardanelles* and *Lucerne*. In a sale of his works after his death there were drawings of the Danube and the Rhine, Malta and Capri, but it is impossible to say how many of these drawings were done from other people's sketches. Captain Hotham (later Admiral Sir William Hotham KCB) provided his own sketches for two views that Carmichael painted in later years; one, *The Great Harbour of Malta from the Corradino Point,* was exhibited at the British Institution in 1855 and

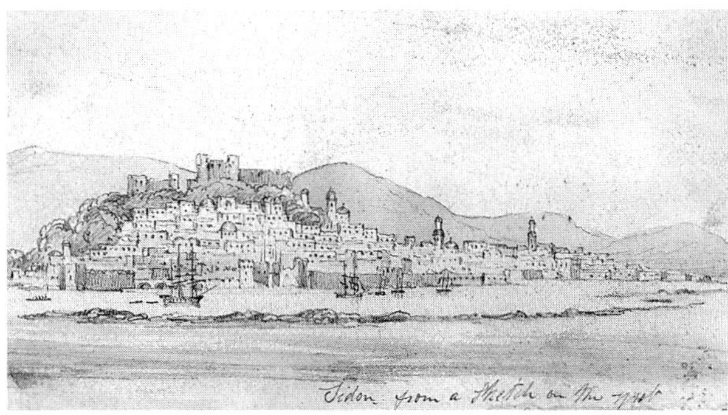

Sidon from a sketch on the spot.
Private Collection.

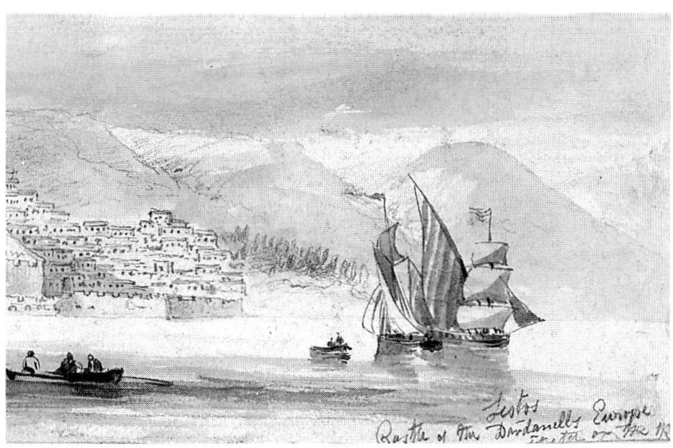

Castle of the Dardanelles.
Private Collection

another, *Moro Castle – Cuba,* were based on these. A *View of Gibraltar* that Carmichael showed at the British Institution in 1859 was perhaps a difficult composition to work up to exhibition standard from someone else's sketch and we know that Carmichael was himself off the Spanish coast during the war years. But unfortunately, except for his time in the Baltic, we have no dates for Aaron Watson's reference to "frequent travels".

It is more than likely that two of the countries to which Carmichael travelled first would have been Holland and Italy. A picture he exhibited in 1826 at the Northumberland Institution was called *Dutch shipping – Flood Tide*, and in 1829 he painted *Dutch Galliot off Sunderland* and exhibited *Dutchmen going into Port – Morning*. But he could have borrowed sketches for these, for most of the marine artists were influenced by the works of the Dutch artists, and he would also have seen Dutch boats fishing off the English coast.

THE INFLUENCE OF DUTCH AND ITALIAN MARINE ARTISTS.

The Dutch tradition had taken root over a century earlier when the best known Dutch marine artists, Willem Van de Velde and his son,[2] also Willem, had come to London in the winter of 1672-3. With the French invasion of the Netherlands in May 1672, a number of artists and craftsmen chose to take up residence in England. Charles II even issued a declaration encouraging Dutch people to settle here and the King was especially pleased to acquire the services of the by then famous Van de Veldes.

So by the 19th century British artists had seen many paintings from Dutch artists showing Dutch craft such as galliots, koffs and fishing pinks and the British wanted to see the country from which they came. They were encouraged to by famous past and contemporary artists. Sir Joshua Reynolds[3] advocated that "Painters should go to the Dutch school to learn the art of painting as they would go to a Grammar school to learn languages". Turner[4] is reputed to have said, when studying a Van de Velde[5] sea piece, "This made me a painter". And E.W. Cooke,[6] who some experts consider was one of the most accomplished and versatile of all the marine artists working in England in the second half of the 19th century, freely admitted he was inspired by the work of Van de Velde the Younger and even adopted the signature 'Van Kook' as a tribute to the great Dutch master.

This Dutch influence brought with it a wider interest in sea and coastal pictures and during the latter half of the 18th century, as Britain acquired possessions around the world and strengthened her command of the sea, the number of marine artists increased. Some landscape artists turned to the sea for their pictures as many buyers with no real interest in ships started to enjoy living with marine subjects and views. If they were not actually dependent on the sea for their living, many travelled along the coast by boat or were beginning to take their holidays on the coast. As David Cordingly[7] writes "..... storms and shipwrecks were as much a part of people's lives then as are road accidents and air disasters today".

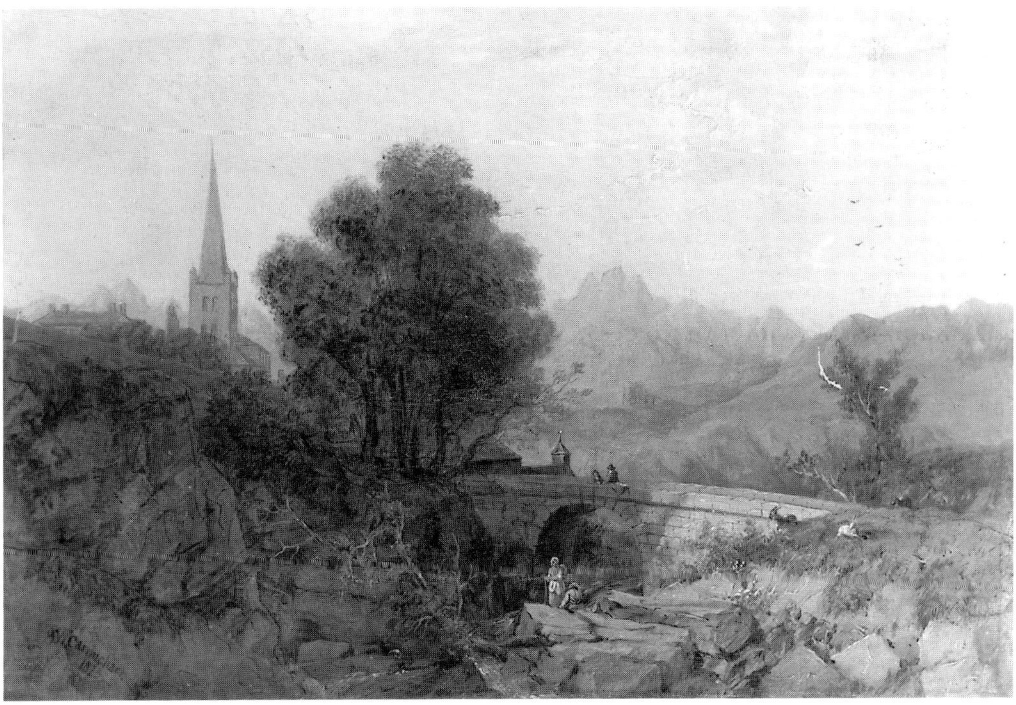

A mountainous Italian landscape. *Sotheby's, London*
Painted when Carmichael was 24 years old.

The Italian influence was also there and many marine artists studied Canaletto.[8] Both Girton[9] and Turner had been affected by him and, in September 1828, the Newcastle artists had a chance to see for themselves when the new Northern Academy held an exhibition of Old Masters. There were a number from the Dutch school and works by Salvator Rosa,[10] Titian[11] and Canaletto were also on view. Most of these exhibits were loaned by wealthy Patrons of the area. Two Canalettos came from the collection of a local man of influence, Major Anderson, who probably commissioned a picture Carmichael painted in 1829 and exhibited in 1830 called *Ascension Day on the Tyne*. In this Carmichael certainly shows that he approached this composition with Canaletto in mind and it presumably pleased Major Anderson who later bought more of Carmichael's work. The Major's death in 1831 was a loss to the Northern artists.

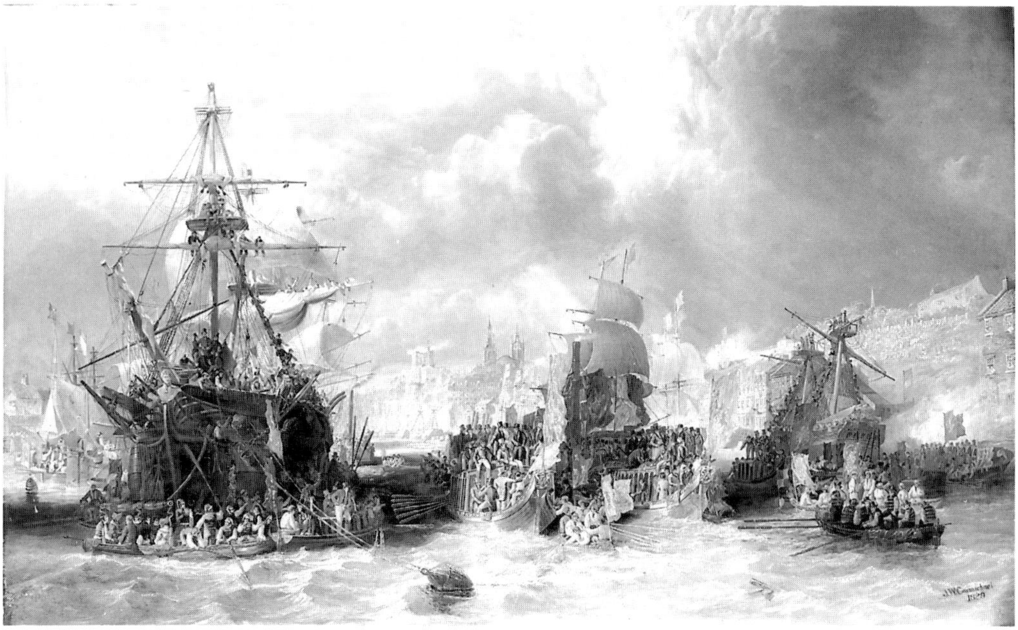

Ascension Day on the Tyne.

Bowes Museum Private Collection

This was the day the Mayor and Burgesses surveyed the boundaries of the River Tyne

SECOND PUBLICATION

Carmichael used this painting for his second step into publishing and it was engraved as a plate in a series of engravings and etchings from sketches that he did of the river Tyne. Between 1828 and 1830 these were issued in six parts called *Views on the Tyne*, each part containing four prints. *Ascension Day on the Tyne* was the first in part two. *The Northern John Bull* reviewed them in September 1829 saying, "..... the excellent views on the Tyne now publishing ..... beautifully engraved by Collard." Thirty two pictures were prepared but for some reason not all were used.[12]

William Collard[13] was one of Newcastle's most prolific engravers and he occasionally collaborated with another local engraver, Mark Lambert.[14] Over the years Carmichael was to produce so many drawings for Lambert that he was frequently described as the latter's "chief draughtsman".

The Newcastle and Gateshead Directory for 1833 have an address for the Carmichaels at 4 Ravensworth Terrace, Gateshead as well as at 20 Blackett Street, the Northern Academy of Art. It also shows that William Collard was next door at number 5. Carmichael's house has been reconstructed in the Beamish, the North of England Open Air Museum in County Durham – it is now the dentist's house in Town Street!

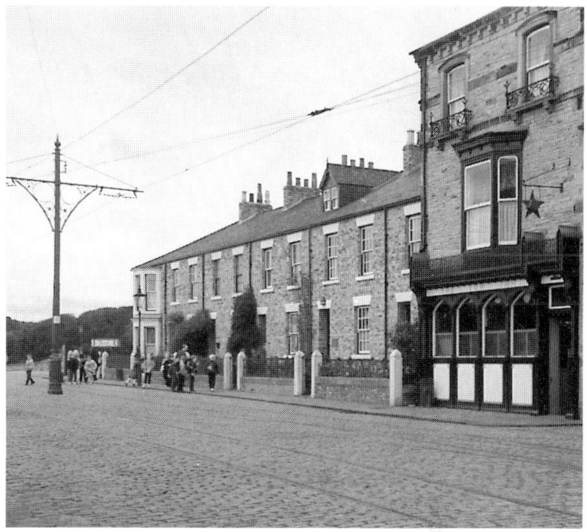

"4, Ravensworth Terrace"
Photographer Myrna Hall
Carmichael's house has the dormer window

With the publication of *Views on the Tyne* Carmichael was slowly developing into a well liked and respected artist. There were at that time several artistic societies established in Newcastle and as Richard Welford points out in his *Men of Mark* "Carmichael was a member of them all". It was perhaps lucky for the artist that the art reviewers, for the most part, approved of his work. In 1829 when the exhibition of the Northern Academy opened, the reviewers produced a booklet criticising all the artists' work and Carmichael came out quite well.

ART REVIEWS

For his *Dutchmen going into Port – Morning,* exhibited in 1829, he was congratulated on "A pretty morning effect ..... The effect of the sun upon the water – the waves, as it were, dancing in the radiance – the breadth and the spirit of the darker part of the sea, and the natural look of the distance, make this one of Mr. Carmichael's best paintings .....". His picture, *Vessels on a Sand Bank – Misty Morning* showed his effect of the mist upon the sun, the sky, the distant vessels, the sea near the horizon, and the ship on the sand herself – "delightfully natural". And to even up the criticisms, while the reviewers complimented him on his painting of *Fishermen off Holy Island*, they did think that "the sea has a jaundiced look which is not as it should be".

Of course it would be totally misleading to let anyone think that Carmichael's paintings were the only ones out of the near three hundred exhibits to receive such recognition. Far from it. Most of the artists received encouragement and there was a simple reason for this. A lot of the art reviews were written under noms de plume, two of which were Zanetti and Algarotti and both these names were in real life William Carey, a picture dealer, art critic and champion of local art. Carey himself admits to this in his *Observations on the Primary Object of the British Institution*[15] which he wrote to promote art in the North, (in London he used the name 'Lorenzo' for his reviews [16]). He was well aware that ambitious artists would always be thinking of leaving Newcastle for some other centre, most probably London or Edinburgh, so he supported the existence of the Northern Academy. It was probably with this in mind that in September 1829 he asked Carmichael to write an official letter of appreciation (he does mention that he had heard Carmichael say that he intended to do so!) and so the following letter appeared.

Blackett Street

Sept 23, 1829

"Sir

I am glad to have an opportunity of acknowledging the great benefit which I have derived from the sight of pictures painted by the best of the British Masters, and those pictures, I feel aware, I would not have seen had it not been through the medium of the Northern Academy of Arts; to which, and to the previous exhibitions of Mr. Richardson's Gallery, I attribute the advance I have made in the Fine Arts, with also the opportunity of offering my own productions for sale.

I am, Sir
Your obedient Servant,

J.W. Carmichael"

One thing can be certain; Carmichael wrote this letter with complete sincerity for without the chance of seeing other works of art and the chance of showing his own he would never have got as far as he did in those first years. It is time to take a look at his painting technique.

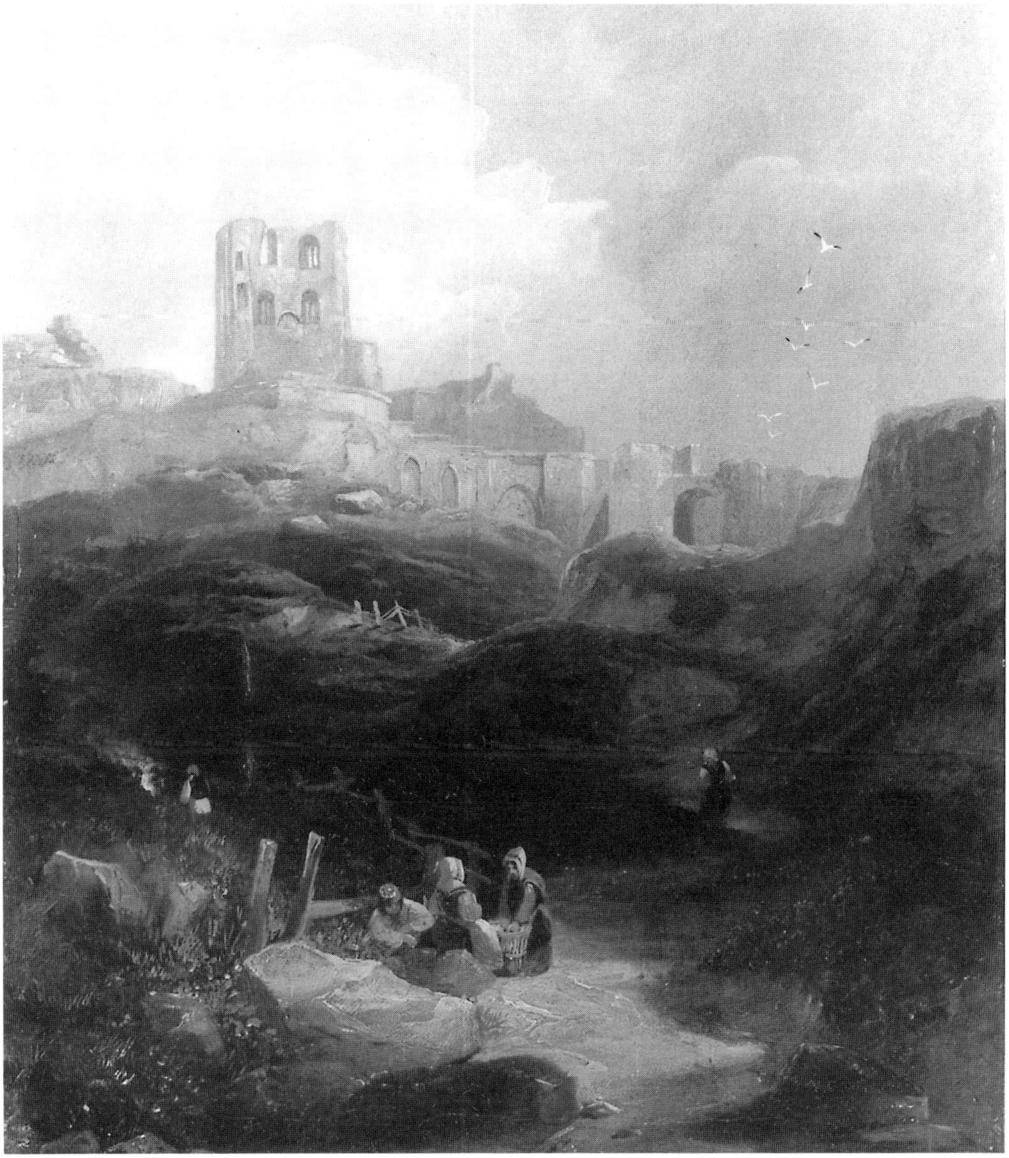

Scarborough Castle in the 1820s. *Scarborough Art Gallery*
This was one of Carmichael's very early oil paintings

Five

PAINTING TECHNIQUE

We can follow Carmichael's methods in two small books that he himself wrote for students, *The Art of Marine Painting in Water Colours* and a companion volume *The Art of Marine Painting in Oil Colours*[1] In the preface of the former he says that the rules he offers for their guidance are drawn from his own experiences of spending long hours not just in big ships but also " ..... in herring boats and cobles of the north, as well as the dainty yachts of the south of our island and indeed every variety of craft".

He suggests that the beginner should direct his attention to sketching objects such as pieces of rock, sea weed, rusty iron, old timber and pieces of wreck for " ..... sometimes the most beautiful points of form and colour in a picture are found in minor accidents". How often we see figures, old buoys, posts and even broken baskets and birds used by most marine artists to support the principal group, though perhaps Carmichael used seagulls more often than most!

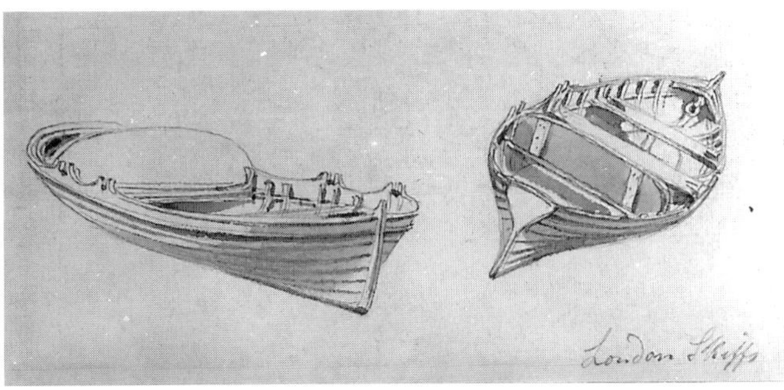

London Skiffs.
Laing Art Gallery, Newcastle upon Tyne (Tyne & Wear Museum)

Again like other artists Carmichael stresses the importance of building up a reference library of sketches for so often the subjects are moving too quickly, but when they are moored they can be sketched on the spot. A "useful memoranda" he calls it and it is sad that we have none of his early sketches though later ones still appear at fine art sales. However the Laing Art Gallery in Newcastle holds hundreds of them that were done in the 1830s and 40s, some of them of craft that have now disappeared. From these we know that he used various sizes of sketch books and different coloured paper in shades of grey, brown and blue feature in the collection. Some are also different views of the same vessel; some even have their rigging diagrams, which shows how carefully Carmichael studied each craft before committing it to canvas. The extent of this "useful memoranda" can be realised when one looks at the catalogue of his studio sale after his death when over 1000 sketches in pencil, sepia and indian ink were sold.[2]

As he writes in his book "..... the difficulty is the outline, if this be not true no trick can hide the inaccuracy". A glance at these examples shows us Carmichael's outlines to be perfect. This attention to detail can be seen on some of his descriptive drawings of various types of ships, some local, some foreign which would have been drawn from the subject itself or from ship's models that Carmichael would have seen from his earliest days in the shipbuilders yards.

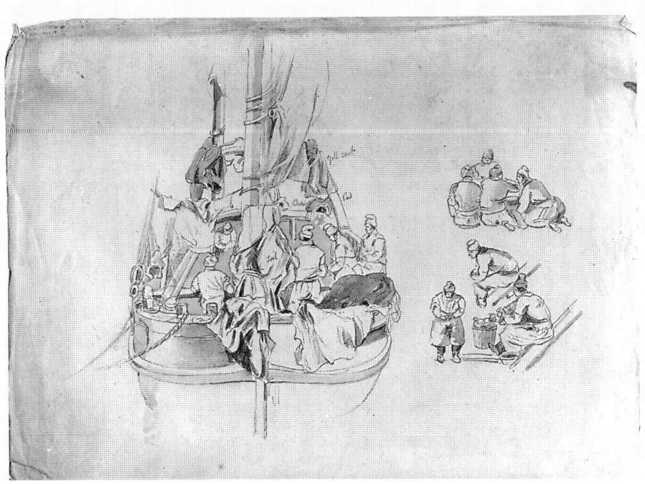

Studies of Fishing Boat and Fishermen.
Laing Art Gallery, Newcastle upon Tyne (Tyne and Wear Museum)

From the first sketches the picture is built up into a composition and one is led to believe that he enjoyed building up his pictures from his studies, one can see him playing with a set of compositional themes. Frequently there is a lot of humour and understanding in the forefront of his paintings, but he reminds the student that "The story of the picture must be in great measure written in the shapes of the clouds and the forms of the sea".

His time at sea and his training as a carpenter held him in good stead and he talks as a sailor and a draughtsman about the proportions of ships and the placing of them in the water. The proportions of the masts of a three-masted vessel are found by taking "the length and breadth of the ship, add them together, and half of that result should be the full length of the main-mast, from its step in the kelson (keelson) to the cap or mast-head". He continues with similar calculations for the other masts, and in case the art student is not himself a sailor there is a diagram to help him.

He gives rules for the correct angle of laden vessels at sea to show the line of wave and the line of flotation. "Dutch traders, colliers, Humber keels, and Thames barges are generally so heavily laden as to reduce their buoyancy to a minimum; and this is seen by the waves passing over their decks fore and aft, as if they were but floating timber or drifting wreck. Buoys, casks and all similar empty bodies float high in the water". With this observation one can understand just how Carmichael manages to make his vessels look as if they are sailing through the water rather than sitting on top of it.

When it comes to manipulating the paper to be used for the final work, every artist has his own methods and we know that Carmichael used a first wash of light red, let it dry thoroughly and than washed it off again with a flat, soft camel hair brush. This he repeated several times until the paper "becomes more manageable and agreeable to work on". If the painting was representing rainy, foggy or stormy skies and seas he covered the paper with uniform washes and ensured that the tone of the wash at the horizon was more aerial than that in the upper part of the sky and the forefront of the painting. To obtain rolling clouds he wetted the paper in the desired shapes and, while the water was still on, he gently removed the surface of the paper with a large round pointed knife in the precise forms which he wanted the clouds to assume, and then washed the surface again with the camel hair brush. Once he had the right tone of all the washes he let the picture dry thoroughly and then used a soft, wet sponge to remove some of the light. If it proved necessary to lighten still further he added a little more water to those

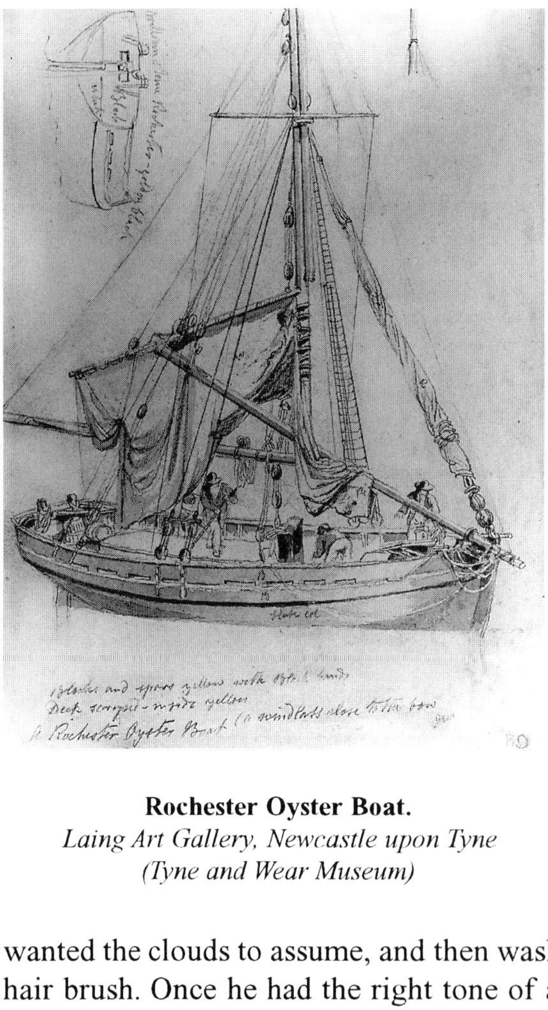

Rochester Oyster Boat.
Laing Art Gallery, Newcastle upon Tyne (Tyne and Wear Museum)

areas, then blotted dry and rubbed up the damp surfaces with a piece of stale bread (a trick that many artists including Turner would have used) or a silk handkerchief, until it came as light as required. Any hard lines around the lightened area he softened with a hog's hair brush moistened in clean water, and then blotted with absorbent paper. He did this anywhere that the picture became too heavy. If he needed to emphasise an area, such as the crests of waves or broken waters in the forefront of the picture, he carefully used a penknife or scraper or, in some cases gentle strokes of Chinese White.

The late 1820s were Carmichael's formative years, his development was rapid and by 1835 he was painting with confidence. As can be seen in a large picture of *Newcastle from St. Ann's* he has obeyed all his own rules of composition (see colour plates). The groups of ships are well connected and kept together in effect and yet they are individually distinct; there is one group (the near one) more striking than the others and the tone of the wash at the horizon is more aerial than the tone of the wash in the upper part of the sky. The winding river Tyne just disappears into the sky. And look at the human touch; those figures with their immature faces (and the broken basket) – the 'minor accidents' – to fill in the waste ground on the right. In the opinion of the Laing Art Gallery this is the finest Carmichael watercolour that they possess and was used as a catalogue cover for an exhibition of the artist's work in the 1982 Newcastle Festival.[3] His greatest critic would have to agree that it shows his draughtsmanship to be impeccable and his colouring sensitive.

It is a view of the city and Gateshead looking from the east about a quarter of a mile from where Carmichael was born. Both Girton[4] and Turner[5] had previously painted the same view, Turner in 1823 from the exact spot. Was this one of the reasons why Carmichael chose to do the same? We have heard how he shared his admiration for the works of Turner with many, not all, of his contemporary artists and certainly in the 1820s Carmichael was referring to him and this interest continued all through his life. In 1855, after admiring a night sky, he wrote in a journal[6] "The stars looked like diamonds set in pearl. Bright as gems but strange no dark contrast" and then suddenly continues, "Turner is more like Nature, the more I see of Nature the more I esteem him" and a few weeks later when Carmichael is trying to describe the moon and decides that any artist would have difficulty ..... "except old Turner" and again repeats "the more I see of Nature the more I think of that great man ....."

Turner had died four years before Carmichael wrote those words of appreciation which were written far from home in a war atmosphere, so he must have had the artist well imprinted on his mind. We are perhaps tempted to speculate that when writing them Carmichael had been quoting the author and critic John Ruskin who said that "when he examined Nature he found so frequently her reflection in Turner".[7] And in 1859 in his handbook for students Carmichael is reminding the would-be artist of the need to keep background and accessories subordinate to the main object or effect. "As an instance of how beautifully this may be effected in the treatment of seas and skies", he writes, "we would refer him to many of the works of Turner wherein the distant ships are made to mingle with the stormy sky".

Carmichael's admiration for Turner's work continued even when the latter's seascapes ceased to be traditional and became more symbolic, using sudden and bright colours to achieve his dramatic effects. This technique was in direct contrast to the majority of Carmichael's marine work who always brought a naturalness to his seascapes by manipulating the effects of sunlight and shadow to contrast light and shade, thus achieving a result far more detailed than Turner.

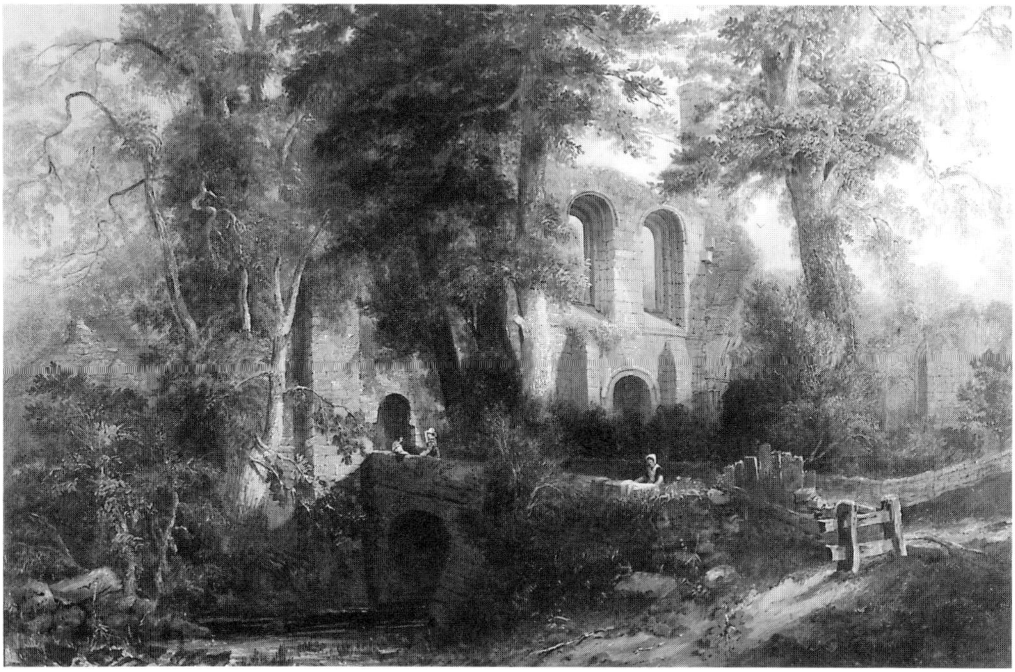

Chapter House, Fountains Abbey.
Private Collection. Bowes Museum, Co. Durham

We have been talking of Carmichael with regard to his marine painting but it must be remembered that in the 1820s and 1830s half of his work consisted of landscapes. Perhaps this was Richardson's influence or perhaps it was the commissions he received, but, as can be seen below, whether he was working with oils or watercolour and in whichever direction his art took him he would always pay great attention to detail. His railway drawings were no exception.

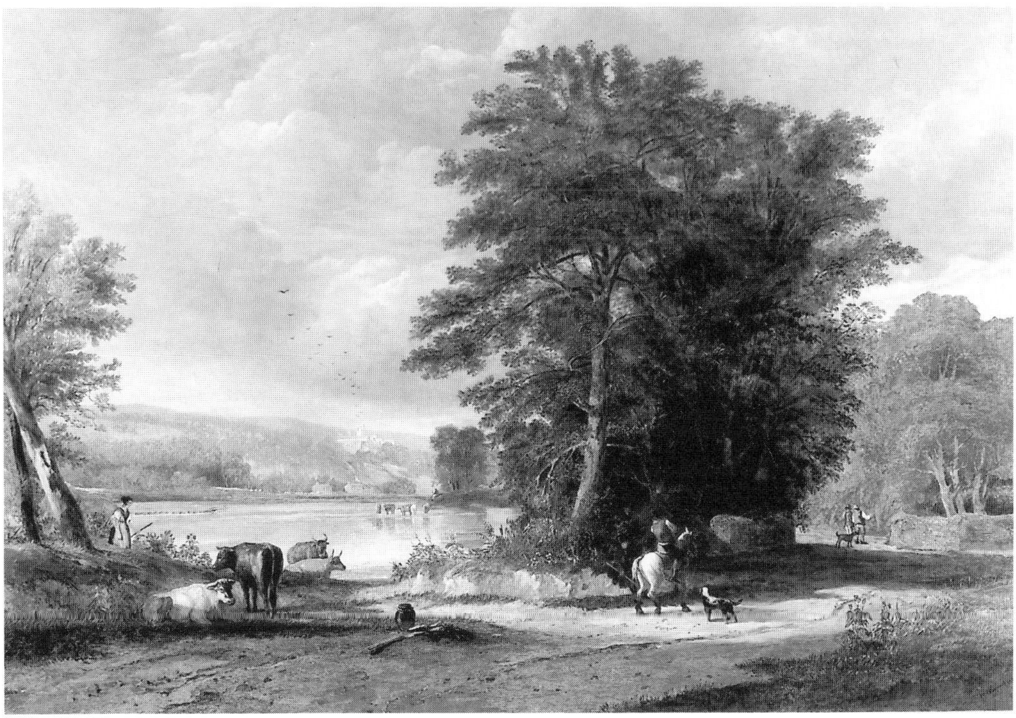

Prudhoe Castle. 1831.

Private Collection. Bowes Museum, Co. Durham

Both these paintings were shown in the Northern Academy Exhibition in 1831.

Six

THE DEVELOPING YEARS

NEWCASTLE AND CARLISLE RAILWAY

The age of the coach had been a short one. It had reached its peak in the 1820s and then began the feverish project of building railways all over the country. The decision to build the first railway line across Britain, from Newcastle to Carlisle, had been made in March 1825, but it was to be another four years before an Act of Parliament was passed and the work could be started. It had to be accepted that the railway had come to stay and would affect everyone.

Carmichael was asked by the Newcastle publishers, Messrs Currie and Bowman, to contribute various drawings for a book that would follow the building of this particular line. Perhaps they were impressed by the way he had prepared his drawings for the engraver in his *Views of the Tyne* series.

The relationship between artist and engraver was a very close one. C.E. Hughes in his book on *Early English Water-Colour* writes of those early engravings[1] and the difficulty an engraver had in representing tone values: "The red in a wall, for example, may be of exactly the same quality, as regards darkness, as the green of a field". So the engraver ..... "could get a better result from a drawing in which the contrasts were produced with a limited range of colours approximating in value to the black and white with which he had to produce his effects". So Carmichael, like most artists working in conjunction with engravers, would produce his drawings in the form of monochrome, and there are a number of these preparatory drawings in collections held by the Laing Art Gallery in Newcastle and the Carlisle Art Gallery.

We do not know how much Carmichael was paid for his 'railway' assignment but the money would certainly have been welcome, for by 1838 when the final drawings were published he and Mary had enlarged their family to six. In 1830, four years after the birth of their first daughter Margaret, came John William (known in the family as Jack). Two years later a second daughter Mary arrived, and was also given her mother's maiden name, Sweet and presumably to avoid confusion was nicknamed Polly. Then in 1834 Annie arrived, to be followed in 1836 by Louisa Balmer (named after Carmichael's artist friend George Balmer) and then, when a second son Benjamin Corbyn was born in 1838, the family were forced to move to a larger home in Newcastle.

12 Ridley Place has been demolished but there are some of the original Georgian houses still there to give an idea of what it would have looked like and old maps show that the houses used to have back gardens. But the Carmichaels probably did not take the whole house for it was quite usual in those days for the less well-off to take rooms or lodgings. All the indications are that they were a happy family. Carmichael referred in his later life to them as such, but with his work output he would have spent more time in his studio than at home and in 1838 he was 'out and about' deeply involved with his railway drawings.

The first section of the Newcastle to Carlisle railway was the seventeen mile stretch between Blaydon and Hexham which was opened in March 1835. Two of the many drawings which Carmichael made in 1836 for a book on the building of the railway were *Cowran Cut looking West* and *Wetherall Bridge looking North by River Eden.*

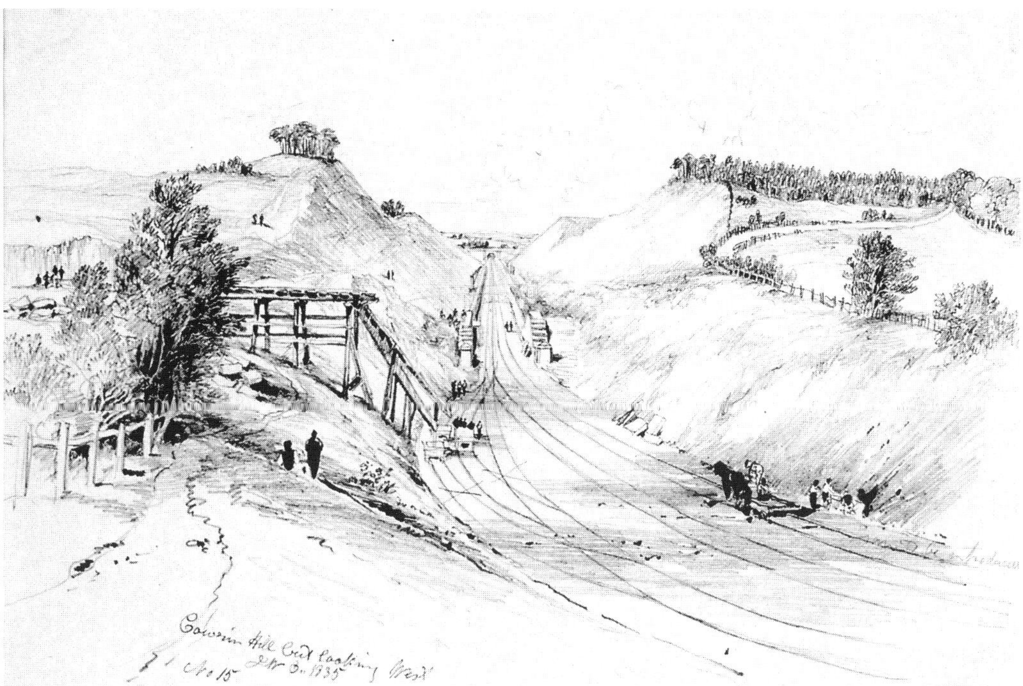

Cowran Hill Cut looking West.
Tullie House, City Museum and Art Gallery, Carlisle

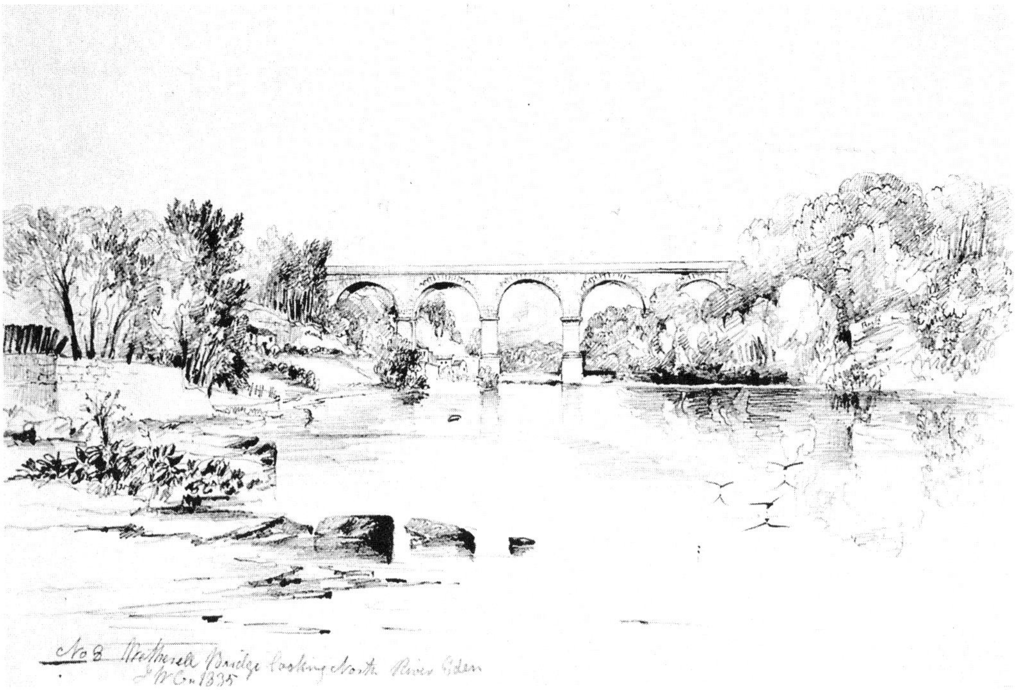

Wetherall Bridge looking North by River Eden.
Tullie House Museum and Art Gallery, Carlisle

Another local artist, Thomas Henry Hair,[2] was also involved with the railway building, but he specialised in industrial pictures, especially those of coal mines, some of which he engraved himself. He also engraved two of Carmichael's railway scenes.

Messrs Currie and Bowman advertised in the 'Newcastle Courant' of 24th August 1838 that they would be bringing the drawings out in a series of six. Each number would contain "four exquisite Line Engravings of the beautiful Spots on that interesting Line of Road, from Drawings by J.W. Carmichael, the Letterpress by John Blackmore, Engineer to the Company. Price of each number, Imperial Quarto before Letters, 6s, Demy Quarto, India Proofs 5s, Prints 3s."

Such prices would hardly have reaped great rewards for the artist, but when the completed railway was opened in May 1839 and the publishers produced the book as a whole, in what was really a second edition, it brought much publicity for everyone concerned, especially Carmichael who through this work was then in touch with 'The Railway Kings'.

PATRONS

From the 1820s Carmichael had had as a friend and Patron a wealthy mining engineer, Nicholas Wood who, in his turn was a friend of George Stephenson, the "Father of the Railways". Either through them or because of the publication of the railway book, Carmichael met two new Patrons, Colonel Stobart who was chairman of the Stockton to Darlington Railway that had opened in 1825, and Mr. George Hudson, M.P.

The Sunderland and Durham Railway was one of Mr. Hudson's schemes and he and Carmichael obviously knew each other over a long period for it was years later that the artist wrote in his journal "Mr. George Hudson, M.P., sent me a cheque for a picture and a very kind note saying he thought the work perfect. Perfection is far beyond my reach. However I was very pleased he liked the picture."[3]

Mr. Thomas Sopwith,[4] the engineer, author and artist, was another Patron of Carmichael's – the two had met when Sopwith was surveying part of the Newcastle to Carlisle Railway. He was four years younger than Carmichael and had many interests and mixed with the most eminent railway and mining engineers of the day. Over the years he commissioned Carmichael to paint many works.

During 1838/39 Carmichael was the guest of the Mitfords in Hunmanby, Yorkshire (not far from Flamborough Head) where he was commissioned to paint at least 20 watercolours of local coastal scenes. Several of these came up for sale direct from the Mitford family in 1947.[5] Another Patron was Lord Bolton who appeared fairly early in Carmichael's career. So did the future Lord Ravensworth, himself an amateur artist, and in the 1840s the 6th Duke of Devonshire commissioned a set of wood panels for Chatsworth of which we will hear more later.

So by the late thirties Carmichael had several helpful and influential friends; he would have needed them for as we have seen the selling prices for paintings in the north were not lavish. Aaron Watson in his memoir quotes Carmichael as receiving prices in the range of thirty shillings to fifteen guineas for his work and goes on to say ..... "but he was an eager and relentless worker and pictures were dispatched from his easel with a rapidity which probably no painter of equal powers has excelled."

It is noticeable in many of Carmichael's pictures, and for that matter with some other self-taught artists such as Nicholas Pocock,[6] that they have an awkwardness when it comes to painting faces. Whenever Carmichael needed the human element his subjects are invariably turned away, or they are looking down wearing wide brimmed hats or his characteristic red woollen caps, other times he just loses the faces in an indistinct mist. A watercolour of *Alnmouth* dated 1833 shows the majority of the figures have their backs turned towards the painter and in a landscape of *Westoe Village* painted in 1838 the one figure that is facing looks like a round bun with currants for eyes! It is in complete contrast to the skill he shows in the sensitive and delicate brushwork of the houses, the trees and the absence of any harsh horizon as the sky drifts down into the distant landscape (see colour plates). And his confidence with the drawing of faces does not appear to have increased with time. Perhaps he comforted himself with the thought that even his idol Turner never got his faces right (John Ruskin author and critic described Turner's faces as looking like "round balls with four pink spots in them instead of faces").

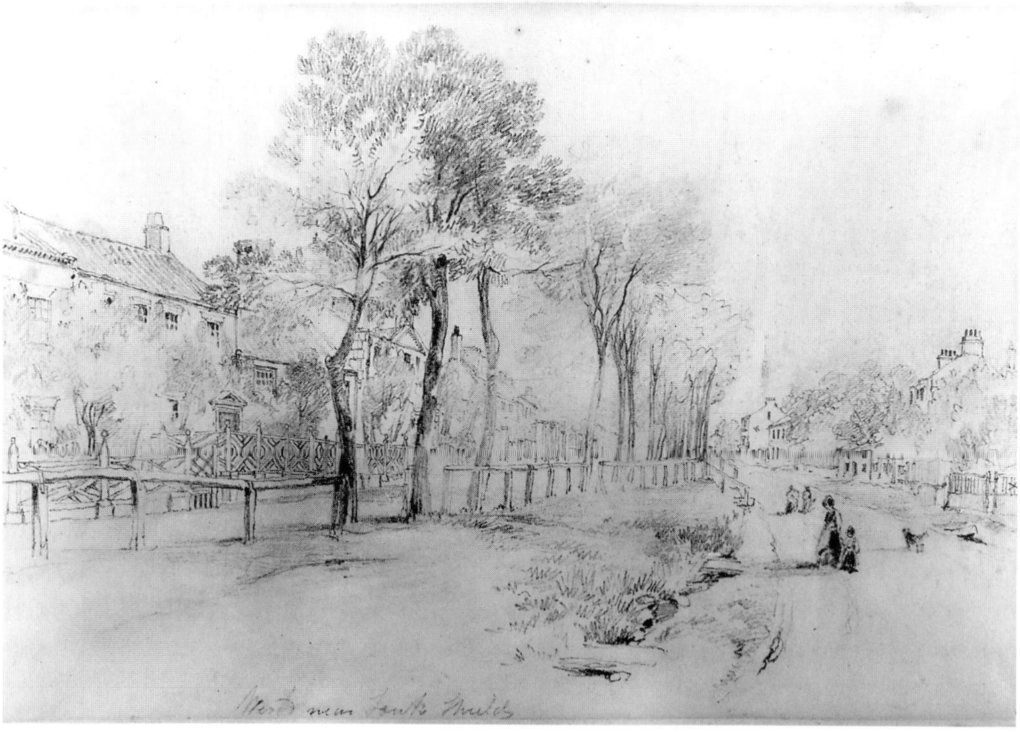

A preliminary sketch of Westoe Village.

South Shields Museum and Art Gallery (Tyne and Wear Museum)

As can be seen from this pencil study, Carmichael made a few changes and additions in his final painting (see colour plates)

Someone who might have helped Carmichael was the artist Thomas Carrick[7] who arrived in Newcastle in 1836, when he was already becoming known for his miniature painting on marble. He had also taught himself to paint. He and Carmichael were about the same age and both had wives named Mary and during the three years the Carricks were in the north a life-long friendship developed.

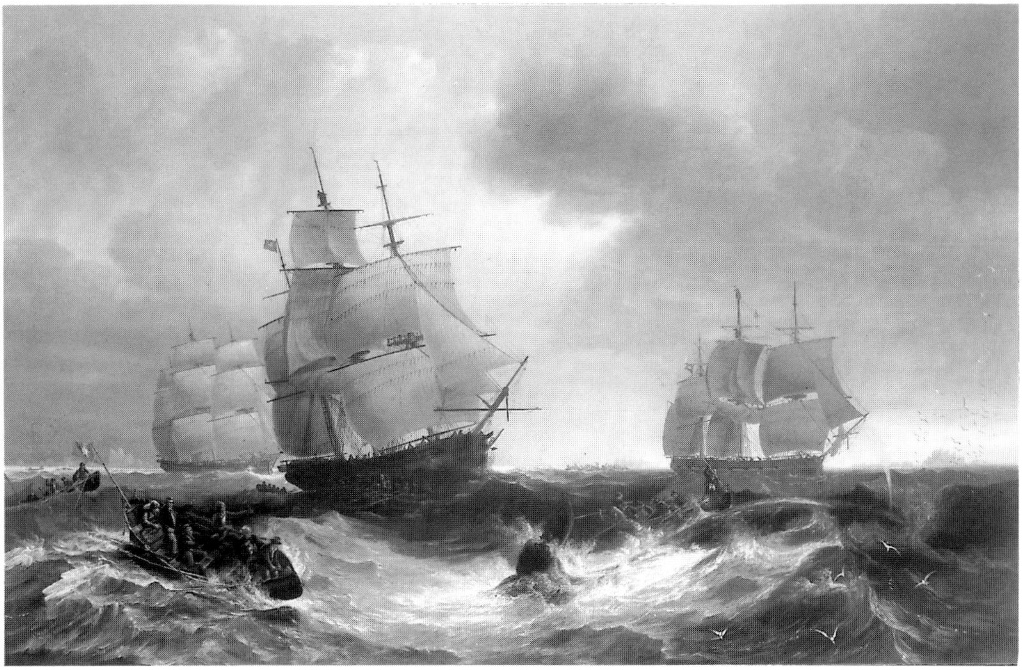

The Newcastle Whaling Fleet. *Omell Gallery, London*

But Carmichael would have had no trouble with faces in the dramatic oil he did in 1835 of the *Newcastle Whaling Fleet.* Since the latter part of the eighteenth century whaling scenes had been a popular theme amongst the marine artists. In the 1830s and 1840s the Newcastle Whaling Fleet consisted of about four vessels and in Carmichael's picture we have his shipping at its best, plus an accurate representation of a typical whaling scene of the period. Every tiny detail is there – the jack flying from the whaleboat shows they are fast to a whale and you can see the man in the stern whose responsibility it is to attend to the whale line. The smaller boats of sailors and the larger vessels are placed in the water at the correct angle for their size and shape. To use his own words –

"the principal group is placed about one third of the length of the composition".[8] It is sad that this picture went to America in 1982 but I am grateful to the Kendall Whaling Museum for allowing me to reproduce it here.

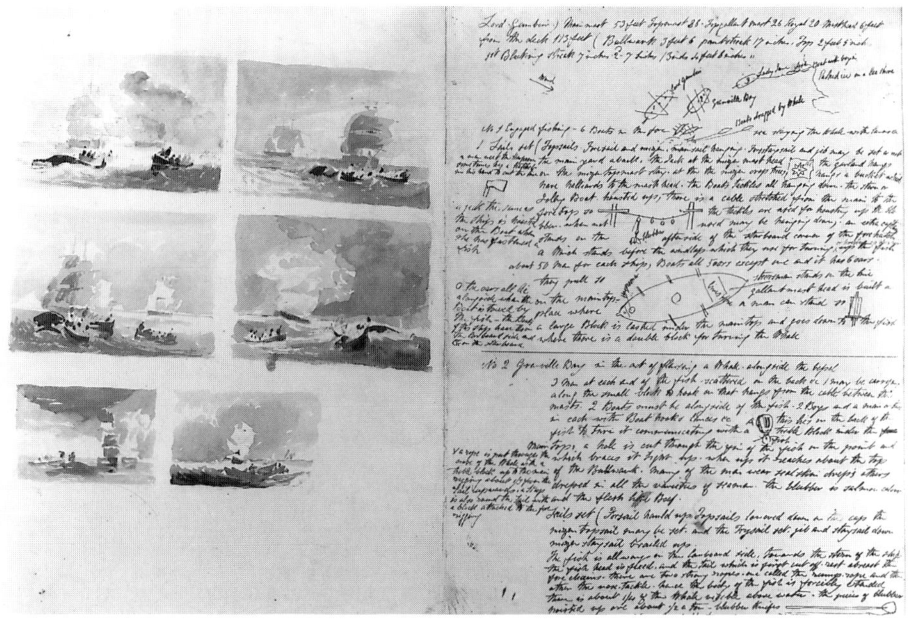

Designs for an arctic picture.
Laing Art Gallery, Newcastle upon Tyne (Tyne and Wear Museum)
This study of whaling ships and arctic views shows the great detail into which Carmichael went for his finished paintings.

FIRST EXHIBIT AT THE ROYAL ACADEMY

So far we have only discussed Carmichael with regard to his local provincial art but in 1835 he must have been delighted to have his first painting accepted for the Royal Academy's Exhibition. At that time the Academy was in Trafalgar Square, though the Square was still but a name to commemorate the Battle. Presumably Carmichael travelled to what was then known as the Metropolis to see his picture – *Saving the crew of a wreck scene, Scarborough Bay* hanging at no: 520. If he was there, he no doubt would have seized the chance to see the exhibits that Stanfield[9] and Cooke[10] and other eminent marine artists had submitted and one of Turners' pictures that year was *Keelmen heaving in coals by moonlight.* This was a view of the industrial Tyne, and one in which Carmichael would surely have taken an interest though, among the various references to Turner, he never mentions that the two ever met.

His exhibit of Scarborough was one of many views that he painted of this seaside town which he enjoyed so much that in 1863 he and Mary retired there.

FIRST EXHIBIT AT THE SOCIETY OF BRITISH ARTISTS

In 1838 he showed a picture in London at the Headquarters of the Society of British Artists in Suffolk Street. The galleries had been founded in 1823, principally for the display of oil paintings, and he exhibited an Italian view *Shipping in the Bay of Naples*. His next exhibit at the Royal Academy was not to be until 1841 with *H.M.S. Conqueror towing H.M.S. Africa off the shoals of Trafalgar, three days after the battle*.

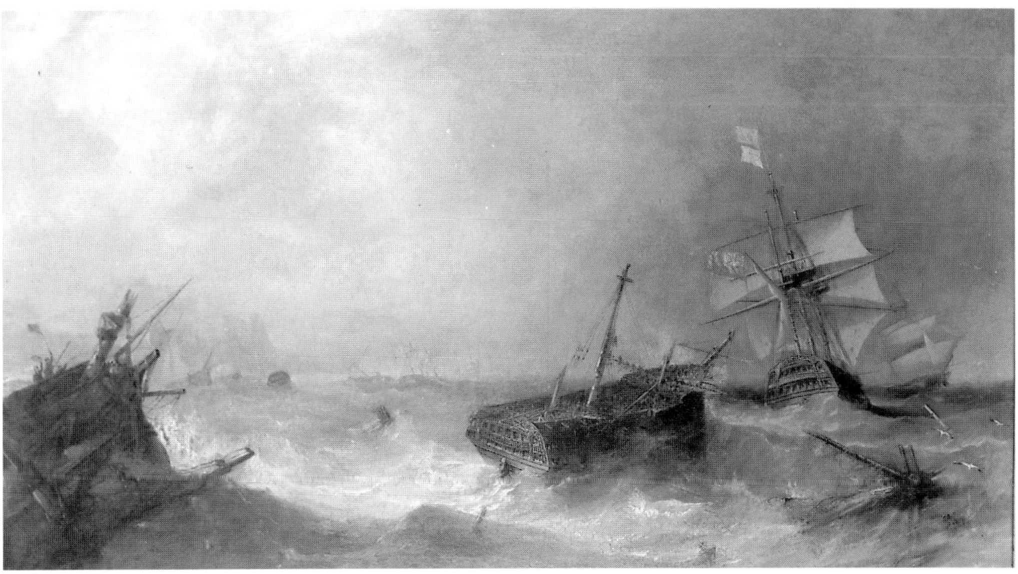

HMS Conqueror towing HMS Africa off the shoals of Trafalgar. *Sotheby's, London.*
Carmichael exhibited this busy scene at the Royal Academy in 1841

It was a small start into the wider art world, but an encouraging one for someone with ambitions who, like many provincial artists in those days was beginning to feel the need to 'try his luck' in London. But there was still much work to keep him in Newcastle and, if it lacked the excitement and challenge that London offered, there were compensations. Take for example the story of the Grace Darling rescue which was to prove a great bonus to artists, especially to those in the north.

THE GRACE DARLING RESCUE

The 'rescue' took place after the ss *Forfarshire*, sailing from Hull to Dundee, was wrecked on one of the Farne Islands, near the Longstone lighthouse on the north east coast of Northumberland. At the risk of their lives the lighthouse keeper, William Darling, and his daughter Grace rowed to the rescue of nine of the crew.

This incident occurred in 1838 when the struggle for female emancipation was just beginning and within days of the event this simple twenty three year old girl found herself committed to the role of national heroine, put there by what we today would call the 'media'. But even without radio and television the news soon reached the world and then all the writers, poets and artists set to work.

Besides Carmichael there were fellow artists Robert Watson,[11] John Reay[12] and Henry Perlee Parker[13] from Newcastle; Robinson Elliott[14] and David Dunbar[15] from South Shields; Edward Hastings[16] from Durham; and George Harrison[17] from Leeds. All of these had a head start on the artists in the south of the country.

As marine artists, several of them including Carmichael were soon to discover that they were up against a problem. The painting of the sea, the storm and the boats was easy enough to portray but the whole point was to show the desperate effort, the femininity of Grace Darling, and the danger she shared with her father, emotions that should show on their faces.

Carmichael's first picture of the rescue was done from the descriptions he had received. It is a typical Carmichael. In the distance he shows the Longstone Lighthouse; the *Forfarshire* is in the middle, lying over on her side with frightened figures clinging to her hull; in the foreground the coble or small open rowing boat shows William Darling in his shirt sleeves and waistcoat. Grace is shown with cropped hair and wearing a short sleeved dress, and both father and daughter have their heads turned away – so there are no facial expressions to bring the story to life! This drawing was one of two water colours that Carmichael was commissioned to paint of the journeys to and from the wreck, and they were sold as lithographs at a guinea each to make money for a 'Darling Fund'.

As time passed the writers and artists went to visit the lighthouse and to hear from the Darlings themselves and they got more accurate details. They talked to Grace and noticed that she had long flowing hair. They saw the dress she had been wearing; that it had long sleeves; that the material was green and white; and her father had not been in his shirt sleeves but in a black jacket.

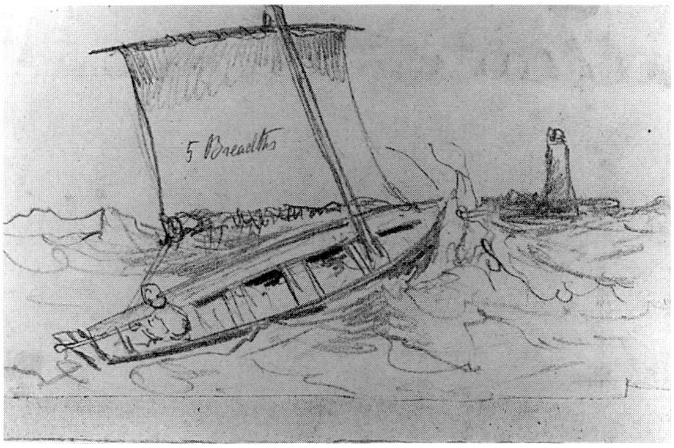

Figure in Coble.
Laing Art Gallery, Newcastle upon Tyne (Tyne and Wear Museum)
Carmichael probably used this sketch of a figure in a Coble going towards the lighthouse for his final painting

How upset Carmichael must have been when he thought of the inaccuracies in his first pictures. He decided that he too must go and see for himself and then do another painting. He also realised that in his first drawing he had made too much of the stricken ship and not enough of the rescuers, for after all this was the part that had captured the public's imagination.

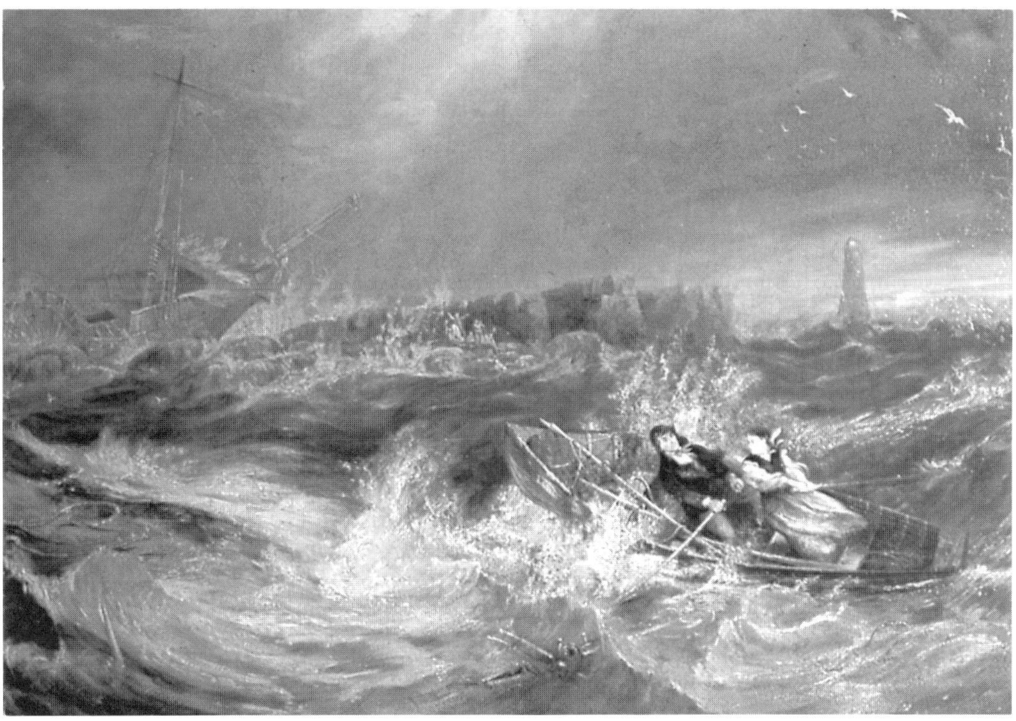

Shipwreck at sea. *Grace Darling Museum, Banburgh*

Perhaps it was Carmichael, or perhaps it was his fellow artist Henry Perlee Parker, a portrait painter, who made the sensible suggestion that they should collaborate on a painting. As the two made their travel plans to go and visit the Darlings, stories reached them that William Darling was somewhat bewildered and was complaining that he and his daughter had already sat for at least seven portrait painters. Carmichael and Parker decided that letters of introduction were necessary.

Parker's letter to Mr. Darling was written by the Newcastle naturalist, Albany Hancock[18] and Carmichael obtained the following letter from the sculptor David Dunbar:

November 7th, 1838

Dear Sir,

The bearer, Mr. Carmichael, is my very intimate friend, and the artist who wrote to me while I had the pleasure of sojourning at your residence, and who made the drawings which are about to be published for the 'Darling Fund'.

Pray show him and our friend Mr. Parker all the kindness you were wont to show me and my companions Watson and Reay and you will again oblige me much. Remember me kindly to Mrs. Darling, Grace and Brooks, and believe me very gratefully.

Yours

D. Dunbar

Written on the back of the letter:

P.S. I should have told you that Messrs C and P are two of the most eminent artists in the North of England and moreover two capital fellows into the bargain.[19]

The final painting captures it all and in it the various mistakes of Carmichael's first picture have been corrected; even the shape of the lighthouse has been altered. Parker's figures have an urgency and a movement that was missing before. There is obvious alarm on William Darling's face and as Grace looks over her right shoulder towards the stricken ship her pale profile mirrors her father's anxiety.

Carmichael and Parker sent this final painting to a London engraver David Lucas. We don't know the reason for not using a Newcastle engraver and it obviously caused the artists extra work for, when the returned proof arrived it had several mistakes which had to be pointed out to Lucas by letter.

Parker wrote that the engraver had caricatured Grace D's chin and "there is a little light beyond the dimple which will be better if it be 'stopped out' so as to make the outline nearly terminate where the dark spot now is". He also had a few criticisms about "Old Mr. D." such as "could not the upper eyelids be darkened a little. It looks at present as if this was the white part of the eye and the eye balls were starting out of the head" and so on.

Carmichael was just as particular as will be seen by the following letter:-

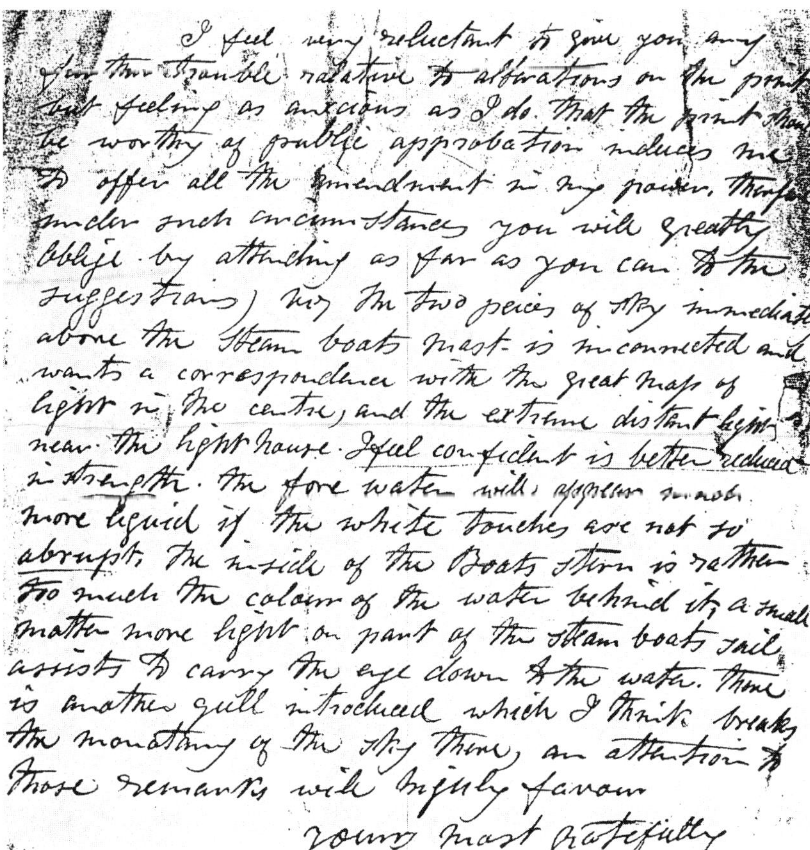

I feel very reluctant to give you any further trouble relative to alterations on the print but feeling as anxious as I do. that the print should be worthy of public approbation induces me to offer all the amendment in my power, therefore under such circumstances you will greatly oblige by attending as far as you can to the suggestions) viz the two peices of sky immediately above the steam boats mast is unconnected and wants a correspondence with the great mass of light in the centre, and the extreme distant light near the light house I feel confident is better reduced in strength. the fore water will appear much more liquid if the white touches are not so abrupt, the inside of the Boats stern is rather too much the colour of the water behind it, a small matter more light on part of the steam boats sail assists to carry the eye down to the water. there is another gull introduced which I think breaks the monotony of the sky there, an attention to those remarks will highly favour

yours most gratefully

J. W. Carmichael

D. Lucas Esqr

Original letter in Laing Art Gallery, Newcastle upon Tyne (Tyne and Wear Museum)

Dear Sir,

I feel very reluctant to give you any further trouble relative to alterations on the print, but feeling as anxious as I do that the print should be worthy of public approbation induces me to offer all the amendment in my power. Therefore under such circumstances you will greatly oblige me by attending as far as you can to the suggestions.

The two pieces of sky immediately above the steam boat's mast is unconnected and wants a correspondence with the great mass of light in the centre, and the extreme distant light near the lighthouse I feel confident is better reduced in strength. The fore water will appear much more liquid if the white touches are not so abrupt. The inside of the Boat's stern is rather too much the colour of the water behind it, a small matter, more light on the part of the steamboat's sail assists to carry the eye down to the water. There is another gull introduced which I think breaks the monotony of the sky there. An attention to these remarks will highly favour.[20]

Yours most gratefully

J.W. Carmichael

CARMICHAEL AS A PERSON

Both these letters were dated 13th May 1839, some months from Parker and Carmichael's visit to the Darlings, so they give an insight into the amount of detailed work that goes into a large painting if it is to be a true reminder of a noteworthy event. It was the type of scene that Carmichael enjoyed painting and he obviously filed his sketches carefully away for he did another version in 1856. It also gives us an insight into Carmichael as a person – the friendly way that Dunbar introduces him to Darling as being "one of the most eminent artists in the north and a capital fellow into the bargain". In his Autobiographical Notes, Bell Scott[21] writes that Carmichael was "bluff and generous; had a considerable library and a hospitable board. Indeed I scarcely expected to find an artist (not a portrait painter) having a household so well appointed as his was, and a friendlier and more honourable man it would be difficult to find".

The reference to the "considerable library" is interesting bearing in mind Carmichael's humble start in life, but he developed a great interest in books and when forced to sell some before his move to London, the titles give us an inkling of these interests; included among many were *Voyages of Cook*, Buchanan's *Scotland* and Knight's *Pictorial England*.

A further indication of Carmichael's popularity was the fact that, after having met William Darling, the two men quickly became friends and on his return Carmichael sent him some books. On the 27th December Darling confirmed the arrival of "a valuable lot of books .... I have not had time to overhaul them yet but I see you have not forgot that Histories, Voyages and Travels is favourites of mine". Two years later Carmichael was still on sufficiently intimate terms with Darling to ask him if he would take "a young Newfoundland dog to train for his friend Mr. William J. Forster?" Considering where the Darlings lived it is not surprising that the offer was turned down as Darling explained that the house he lived in was "not like one's own ..... I can make signal any day for provision of water for myself and family but not for Doggs".[22] And again he thanks Carmichael for some books, presumably another lot?

There are also indications that Carmichael had a good sense of humour (perhaps the latter story was a joke!), but in future anecdotes we get the impression that he had a great sense of fun. Certainly the portrait that Thomas Ellerby[23] painted in 1839 shows a friendly person with eyes that are verging on a twinkle and a mouth that might any moment make a comical remark.

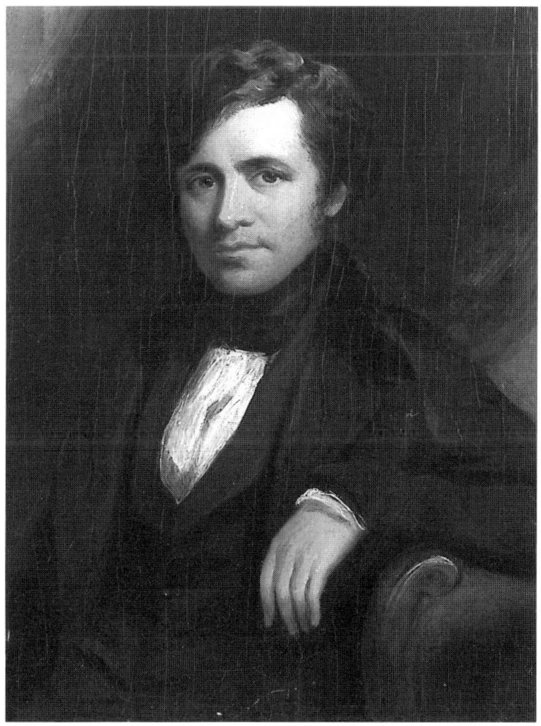

John Wilson Carmichael.
Painted by Thomas Ellerby 1839.
Laing Art Gallery, Newcastle upon Tyne
(Tyne and Wear Museum)

William Bell Scott's reference to Carmichael's "hospitable board" is obviously correct. When we read in a journal he kept in the 1850s all the details of the food he ate, we can see that he obviously found the subject interesting. On June 25th 1855 on board HMS Caesar "..... We had an excellent dinner with good wines and tastey desserts. I liked a wine called Barsac. .....". And on July 8th

1855 again on board HMS Caesar there was a dinner party where ".... the Mutton, the Ham and all the animal requisites were first rate, the Plum Puddings, pancakes, rice rarities and the Veal were all excellent. I enjoyed myself heartily ....." He even wrote down two recipes of `Ship Puddings' for his daughter Annie when on June 5th 1855 he tells how to make a `Rice Pudding' and another called `Hour Pudding'.[24]

He also enjoyed a 'good smoke' and he refers to cigars more often than cigarettes. These would sometimes be accompanied by a glass of whisky but more often brandy which, if it was just before he went to bed, he drank with a little water and occasionally a cup of tea at the same time. As Carmichael enjoyed company he obviously got the reputation for his hospitality. Of course the reference to food and drink quoted above are when he was away from home; there is no doubt that within his own family finances had to be carefully watched.

In the 1841 Newcastle census the Carmichaels are still living at 12 Ridley Place but soon afterwards they have a new address. Perhaps it was the arrival of a seventh child, Ellen Dunbar in March 1841, that necessitated the move to 4 Hood Street. This is a light airy street to the east of Grey Street right in the centre of Newcastle. The actual house has gone but those that remain are large.

On the census the names of the family are correct except in the case of Carmichael himself who is written as "George Wilson". The names of two "female servants" appear, Jane Allchurch Cross, aged twenty three and Anne Middlemass, seventeen. Certainly Mary Carmichael would have needed their help as the eighth baby, a daughter Francis (Fanny), arrived in March 1844.

With their latest move Carmichael was at the heart of many of the views of Newcastle that he had been painting, and continued to do so for some time. They were quick to do and brought in much needed money – but how much? In the Newcastle Courant for 24th August 1838, Messrs Currie and Bowman advertised that *A View of Grey Street* executed in the first Style of Lithography, from a drawing by J.W. Carmichael, was available for the price of 3/6d, but there would have been a lot of work in that picture and one wonders with these prices what the artist received. But no doubt the publishers would have sold a number of them as Newcastle was very proud of their newly planned Grey Street with its smart shops, and the best hotels, and at the top the newly erected 135 foot column – the monument to Earl Grey of Howick.

A glance at a much later sale catalogue in 1879 when part of the Thomas Sopwith collection[25] was sold, gives an indication of what and where Carmichael was drawing and painting at the time in Newcastle itself. *Percy Bridge*; *New Bridge over Pandon Dene*, and many names that are still on the maps today.

Far more of Carmichael's scenes were of outside the city and in the above sale, out of the 396 sketches, drawings and paintings, 196 were Carmichael's and most of these were countryside scenes. But then Thomas Sopwith was one of his earliest Patrons and in the sale there was a picture entitled *View of Newcastle, from the river Tyne* and on the drawing Carmichael had written "This view of Newcastle was drawn before I left my business as a Carpenter. 1824 - J.W. Carmichael."

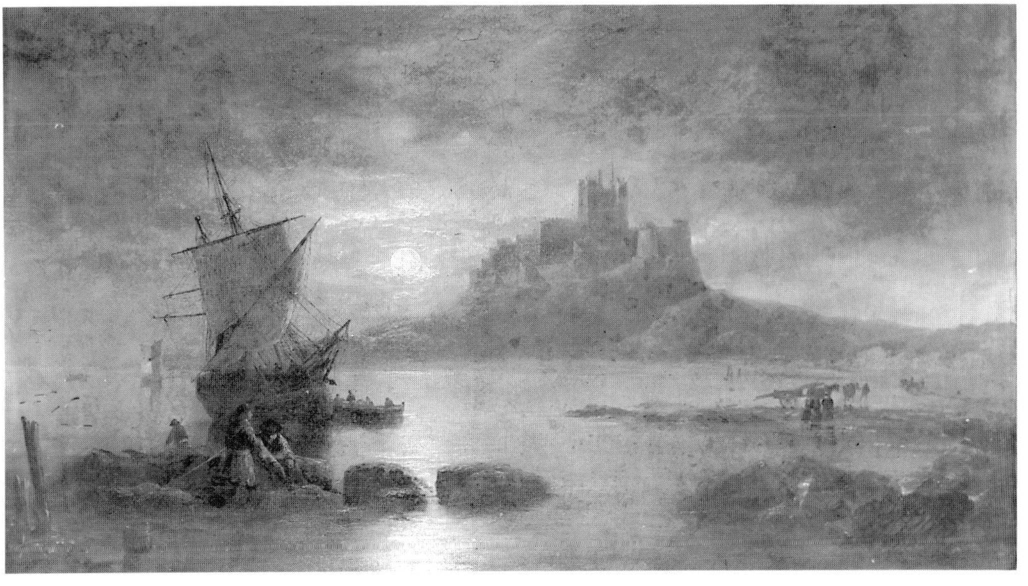

Bamburgh Castle. *Sotheby's, London*

So like most artists, Carmichael was travelling around for his pictures. To mention but a very few: he went north to Alnwick, Holy Island and Bamburgh; west and east for his railway scenes when he did some pictures of a branch of the North Eastern Railway, the Newcastle to North Shields;[26] south to such places as Fatfield on the river Wear where, in the Newcastle Courant for the 24th August 1838, we read that Mr. Carmichael's view of the Victoria Bridge across the river Wear would cost the buyer 4/-; and down the coast to Whitley Bay, Cullercoats, Tynemouth, South Shields, Sunderland and his beloved Scarborough.

But not all the pictures were rapidly executed for quick sale; a number stayed as 'raw material' waiting to be used in compositions for bigger paintings like the scene below.

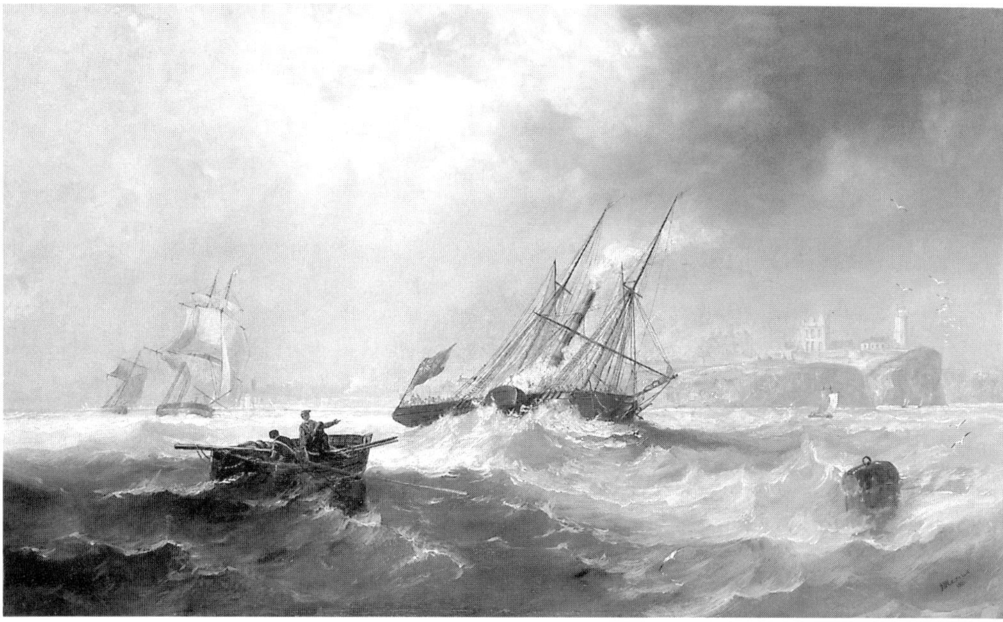

A Paddle Ferry in choppy seas off Tynemouth. 1840.
Old Solent House Galleries, Lymington.
This composition is similar to that on page 16.

ILLUSTRATED LONDON NEWS – THE ARTIST AND ENGRAVER

In 1842 Queen Victoria arrived in Leith in the Yacht *Royal George* for her first visit to Scotland, and her tour was well covered by the *Illustrated London News*. At that time this weekly publication had only been launched three months previously by its Founder, Herbert Ingram, and was the first of its kind in the world: "30 Engravings – Price 6d" announced the advertisement boards. Not surprisingly with a Royal Tour so early in its existence, the *Illustrated London News* ran the event through several editions of its paper and needed a lot of original drawings. So once again the artists gathered.

A number of the finished pictures are unsigned and for that reason I quote Mason Jackson, who was art Editor of the *Pictorial Press* in 1860.[27] "The sketch being completed on paper the services of the draughtsman on wood come into requisition, for it is not often that the drawing on the block is made by the same person who supplies the sketch. Sometimes the sketch to be dealt with is the production of an amateur, or is so hastily or indifferently done that it has to be remodelled or rearranged in drawing it on the wood. Faulty or objectionable portions have to be left out or subdued, and perhaps a point in the sketch that is quite subordinate is brought forward and made to form a prominent part of the picture. All this has to be done without doing violence to the general truth of the representation ....."

ROYAL TOUR

On that particular Royal Tour two artists names appear in the *Illustrated London News* – Ebenezar Landells,[28] a northern wood engraver, and C. Stiff. How many other artists were there we cannot be sure (but we know Carmichael was) because from Delia Millar's publication *Queen Victoria's Life in the Scottish Highlands*[29] we learn that the Queen did not herself have too many pictures of that tour.

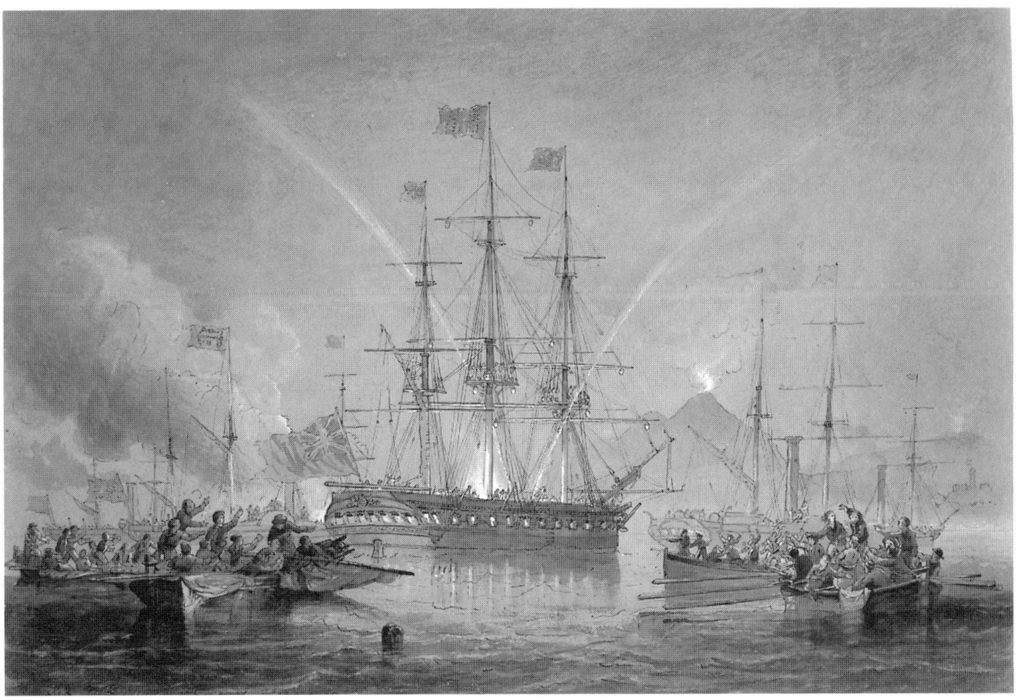

The Royal George arriving at Leith 1842.
The Royal Collection 1994. Her Majesty the Queen.

"After the visit a few drawings were added to the first Souvenir Album, among them two by J.W. Carmichael showing the Royal Yacht in which the party had travelled north ....."

Queen Victoria must have received these watercolours later that year or early in 1843 because that summer Carmichael exhibited at the Royal Academy: *Her Majesty Queen Victoria on board the Royal George Yacht approaching Granton Pier on the morning of the debarkation, September 1st 1842 at 8½ a.m. Painted from a sketch made on the spot and now in the possession of Her Majesty.* The other is *The arrival of Her Majesty Queen Victoria with the Royal Squadron off Edinburgh on the night of Monday August 31st 1842 at 12.0 p.m. Painted from a sketch made on the spot, and now in the possession of Her Majesty.* A view of this is in the York City Art Gallery (see colour plates).

He did several versions of these scenes and one is in the Mansion House in Newcastle. He also did some smaller sepia drawings showing the Royal George off St. Abbs Head, Inchkeith, Leith Roads and Granton.[30]

About this time Carmichael was introduced to the Duke of Devonshire and this involved him in an unusual commission to paint some wood panels in the Oak Room at Chatsworth, and it is clear from the following excerpts taken from the Duke's private handbook dated 1845 that he had fixed ideas as to how the artist was to do them.

> "Not fewer than twenty panels in the wainscoting are occupied by views taken near a fishing village on the coast of Northumberland, that appeared to me last autumn the most enjoyable of places; by name Cullercoates, with glorious sands extending on one side to Tynemouth, and on the north in a range, as secluded as the other side is animated and exciting ..... The sketches are by a sailor become artist, and likely to be eminent, by name Carmichael. To gaze at them is a pleasure, but they recall, or rather make the thoughts turn to, some imaginary groups.
>
> The first – a young girl "clapping youthful hands, wild with emotion" as the waves, unrolling their treasures of light and foam, advance and recede upon the golden sand – Nature's child – unconscious of her inherited talents, of her unsurpassing qualities.
>
> The second – is a matron, seeking on this coast short periods of refreshment and change from the monotony of her peaceful destiny. With a mind full of poetry, and feelings that are not less sublime, she has been bound down by the domesticities of life to an existence that has been serene, that must have been happy, that conquered discontent.
>
> The third – is a grandmother; but, though age is come, her mind retains the

freshness, the charm, the vivid perception of youth. She in vain wraps up her intelligence and warmth in a reserve that only doubles their power when imparted....."

Unfortunately these panels appear not to have survived. In the Oak Room now are four panels, two of pet dogs and two of landscape views, which are unconnected with Carmichael's work.

Another interesting commission came his way in 1846 through his connections with the railways when the Directors of the York, Newcastle and Berwick Railway Company asked him to paint the High Level Bridge over the Tyne. When the last link of the railway between London and Newcastle was finished in June 1844, the line stopped at Gateshead and the passengers had to take a ferry across the river. Five thousand tons of cast and wrought iron went into the construction of a new bridge which was 4,000 feet from the Gateshead station to the Newcastle terminus, and the upper parapet was 130 feet above the bed of the river. To make the assignment more difficult, the Railway

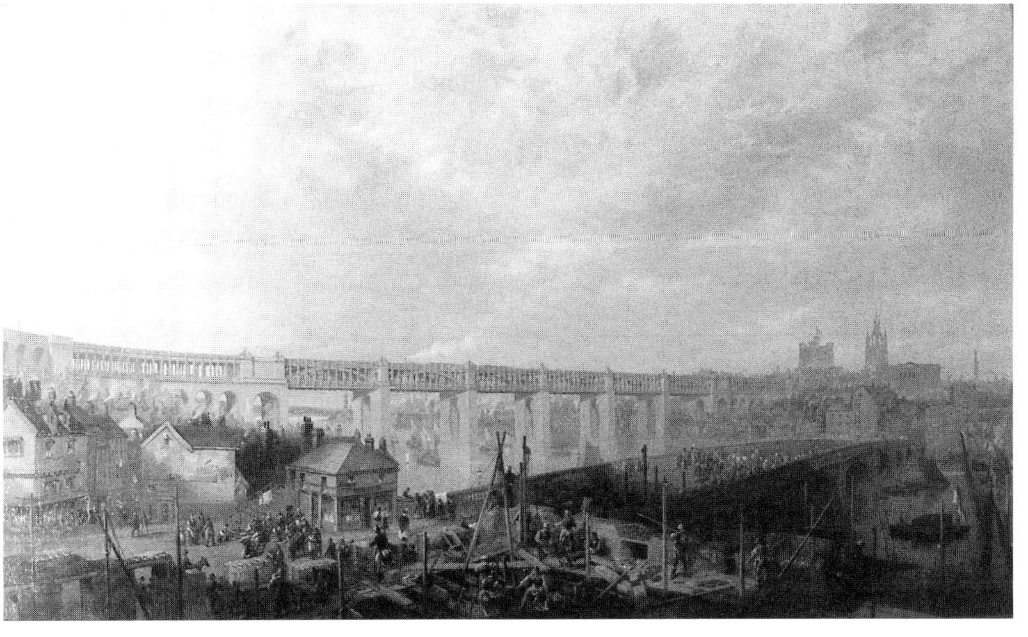

High Level Bridge from Gateshead. *University of Newcastle upon Tyne. Photographer Robin Crampton*

commissioners wanted the painting before the bridge was actually finished so some artistic imagination was needed. A critic in the Gateshead Observer reported "The primary object being a picture of two bridges and there being no vacant site commanding a good view of the two structures, the artist has taken the liberty to pull down (in imagination) the house at the south eastern corner of Tyne Bridge and thus accomplished his design .....". Not an easy task but the Railway Commissioners were delighted with the result, and it hangs today in the University of Newcastle upon Tyne.

So by 1846 Carmichael's work was becoming well known nationally. He had his Patrons amongst the Railway Kings; the Duke of Devonshire was pleased with his work at Chatsworth; he already had two paintings in the Royal Collection; two further pictures *High water at the Harbour mouth* and *Nelson and the Deal boatmen* had both been accepted by the Royal Academy the year before; a second picture *Coastal Scene under the effect of a Snowstorm* had been shown in the Suffolk Street Galleries (the headquarters of the Society of British Artists) in 1843; and 1846 was also the first time he exhibited at the British Institution (this had been established in 1806 in rooms in Pall Mall).[31] So perhaps he was beginning to feel that it was time for a move to London.

The idea may also have been encouraged by Thomas Carrick who was going from strength to strength in the capital with his portrait painting, and was persuading him to 'take the plunge' and move south; or was it just that the more ambitious artists did move there sometime in their working lives? John Martin[32] with whom Carmichael had long been friends was there; Clarkson Stanfield of whom he was slightly envious and on occasions emulated, had left Sunderland and was now famous on the London scene. For whatever reasons, Carmichael decided to move.

His artist friend William Bell Scott, by then Director of the Government School of Design in Newcastle, had himself spent some time in London and knew the pitfalls and tried to dissuade him. But, as he says in his autobiographical notes, nothing would stop him. "..... he would leave the provinces, cut out Stanfield, make his fortune great and his name immortal. So he left us for London."[33]

FAREWELL IN NEWCASTLE

But not before Newcastle had said farewell in style. We can read about the occasion in the Newcastle Courant of 3rd April 1846 when a number of friends "of Mr. John Wilson Carmichael, artist of this town, assembled at Mrs. Walton's, the Exchange Hotel, Grey Street, to present him with a splendid testimonial of their respect and esteem previous to his departure for London. The company was numerous and respectable and included several ladies."

A committee had been formed and the names on it give a clue to the high regard in which Newcastle, especially the church, held Carmichael and his family. It was headed by the Lord Bishop of Durham, the Vicar of Newcastle, and the Reverend Green (a previous Vicar). The Reverend Robert Currie represented Carmichael's publishers and the artist Joseph Crawhall was also on the committee; this may have been the father who was a Sheriff of Newcastle in 1846 or it might have been his son, also called Joseph who did this portrait of Carmichael about that time. Several other local notable names were also included.

The ceremony started with a speech by a Reverend Coxe who said that they had all met together "to testify their interest and respect to the talents and integrity of Mr. Carmichael, and also to declare their admiration of his success as an artist, and their regard for him as an upright and honest man .....". He went on to talk of the way Carmichael "had raised himself to the position he now held, by the innate force of his own genius and character .....". This had been done he continued ..... "without the external aids of birth or artistic education ....." and so on. By the time the Reverend Coxe had gone on to say that "the greater part of Mr. Carmichael's professional career had been among us ..... the bonds that bind you to us, are strong and sacred ....." and it was an easy thing ..... "to transplant the sapling, but the oak of half a century how hard it was to remove ....." emotions were running high. But finally even the Reverend Coxe ran out of words and the presentation took place.

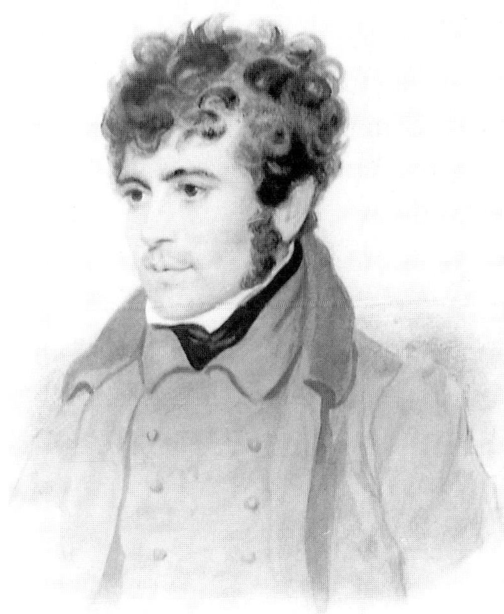

Portrait of Carmichael.
Anderson and Garland, Newcastle upon Tyne.
Painted by Joseph Crawhall the Second, probably in the 1840s.

One report says that the value of the gift came to £145; another £300. Whichever is correct, it was certainly a handsome present and consisted of a silver salver, 12 King's pattern table spoons, 12 dessert spoons, 18 tea spoons, pair of sugar tongs, 4 salt ladles, 1 mustard ditto, 1 sugar spoon, 1 caddy spoon, 2 butter knives, 4 pickle forks, 1 wine funnel, 1 chamber candlestick and 1 cake basket.

After having listened to the Reverend Coxe's lengthy speech, Carmichael was so touched that he had to hand his own reply to his neighbour, the Reverend Dodd, to read for him. "Mr. Vicar and gentlemen of the Committee" Carmichael's prepared speech commenced, and went on to explain how he had never made a speech in public and to beg their acceptance of a plain acknowledgment of his sense of obligation. "..... If ever anyone had reason to be proud of a testimonial, it is myself, as it has been presented by kind friends and patrons who have uniformly fostered and encouraged my humble exertions. Of my own deficiency no one is more sensible than myself .....". He ended with another vote of thanks for his gift and added that – "Mrs. Carmichael begs me to express to you her warmest thanks for the kind way in which you have afforded her so many valuable and useful appendages to her table which I need not say will be always regarded with feelings of pleasure, affection, and gratitude by her and my family. They all join with me in the expression of the deepest gratitude, and in sincere and earnest wishes for the lasting happiness of yourselves and families."

The whole tone of Carmichael's speech was one of humility and gratitude and gives a glimpse into his innermost thoughts. We see a sensitive person, a deep thinking one and, considering the guests present, his religion was important to him. He obviously possessed qualities that endeared him to many people and certainly on that occasion drew admiration from his audience, and when the Reverend Dodd had finished reading, all rose to drink Carmichael's health.

There is another version of this ceremony that came from Bell Scott who describes it this way in his autobiographical notes[34] "..... Two or three hundred pounds were subscribed to present him with silver plate when he left" (the press said it was real silver). "I went to the meeting, when the vicar made a flowery speech, and upset the painter for the moment by his allusion to uprooting the tree from its native soil; but when all the hand-shaking was over and only a few of us left, ladies who had been in the background came to the front, among others the mistress of the hotel (Mrs. Walton) in which the meeting was held. She was a handsome young widow, and when she was handed forward to examine the silver plate, Carmichael, who had quite recovered his spirits, made a dash at her, seized her round the neck, and gave her such a resounding kiss as dispersed the company in a burst of laughter."

These two reports show something of his personality. What of his appearance? Joseph Crawhall the Second's[35] portrait shows him for the first time with side whiskers, and also a suggestion of a moustache, not yet fully matured and which was probably only temporary as it does not appear in later portraits. The eyes have lost the hint of amusement that earlier portraits show (this could have been Crawhall's immaturity as he would only have been in his early twenties at the time he painted this) or perhaps Carmichael was feeling the responsibility of moving his family away to London. Watson mentions in his memoir that Carmichael looked upon the step which he had taken as a serious and even solemn one. "Almighty God" he writes in his journal "I solemnly ask Thy aiding hand that I may be able to keep my family in the comforts of this life".

There is no doubt that his main worry was a financial one. To obtain their travelling expenses Carmichael had to auction some books (mentioned in Chapter 5) and pictures. It would have been a wrench to part with paintings by such artists as David Cox,[36] Crome,[37] Varley[38] and Richardson.[39] Also in the sale were paintings by George Balmer;[40] parting with these would have been especially sad as this life long friend died two weeks after the Carmichaels left Newcastle.

THE MOVE TO LONDON

According to Watson, four days after Carmichael received his presentation of silver he, his wife and eight children ranging in ages from twenty down to two years old were on their way to London by sea. According to the sailing on that Saturday 7th April 1846,[41] they would have boarded the *s.s. London Merchant* whose owners, the General Steam Navigation Company, proudly advertised "that she had recently been fitted with new 200 horse-power engines." It is fun to speculate that perhaps her Master, Captain Stranack would have enjoyed showing his artist passenger, himself a sailor, the engine room. But one thing of which we can be certain – Carmichael would have enjoyed being back at sea and passing all the various places that he and many other artists had painted such as South Shields, Sunderland, Hartlepool, Whitby and Scarborough. The *London Merchant* would then have sailed away from the coast until it was time to approach the mouth of the Thames and then the passengers would soon catch sight of Sheerness to the south. Here were men-of-war and several types of local vessel not usually seen as far north as the river Tyne.

However apprehensive Carmichael must have felt about the move, as an artist he would certainly have been looking forward to painting views of the river Thames. Like the Tyne was to the northern artists, the Thames was a natural base for the southern marine painters. There was a group of artists in Deptford that had been thriving since the early 18th century when Charles Brooking[42] had lived there; artists also gathered in Wapping, Woolwich and Limehouse; and earlier still the Van de Veldes[43] had 'colonised' Greenwich. But there was much to be arranged before Carmichael could again settle seriously to his painting.

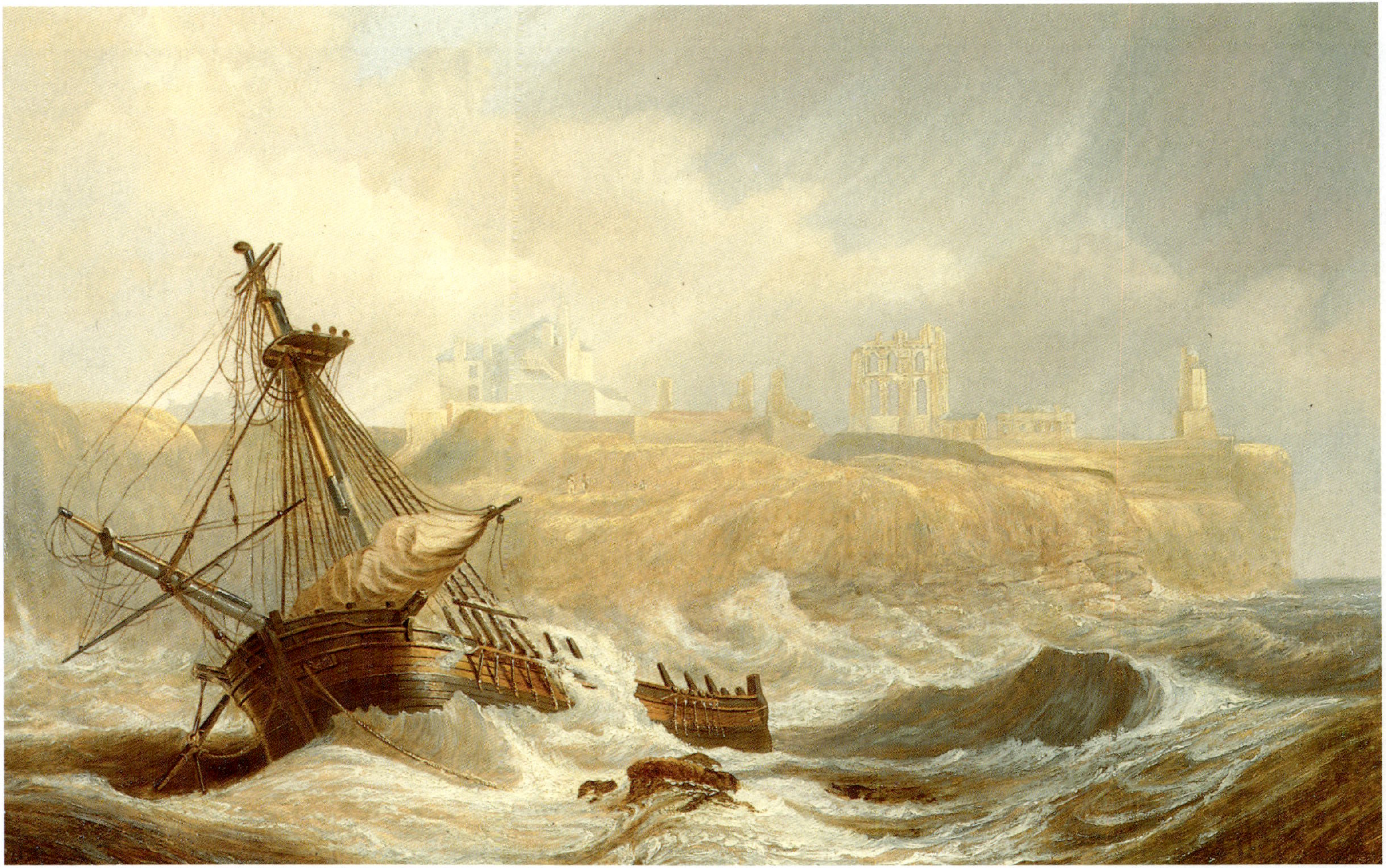

Wreck of the Betsy Cains. 1827. *Private Collection. Dean Gallery, Newcastle upon Tyne*

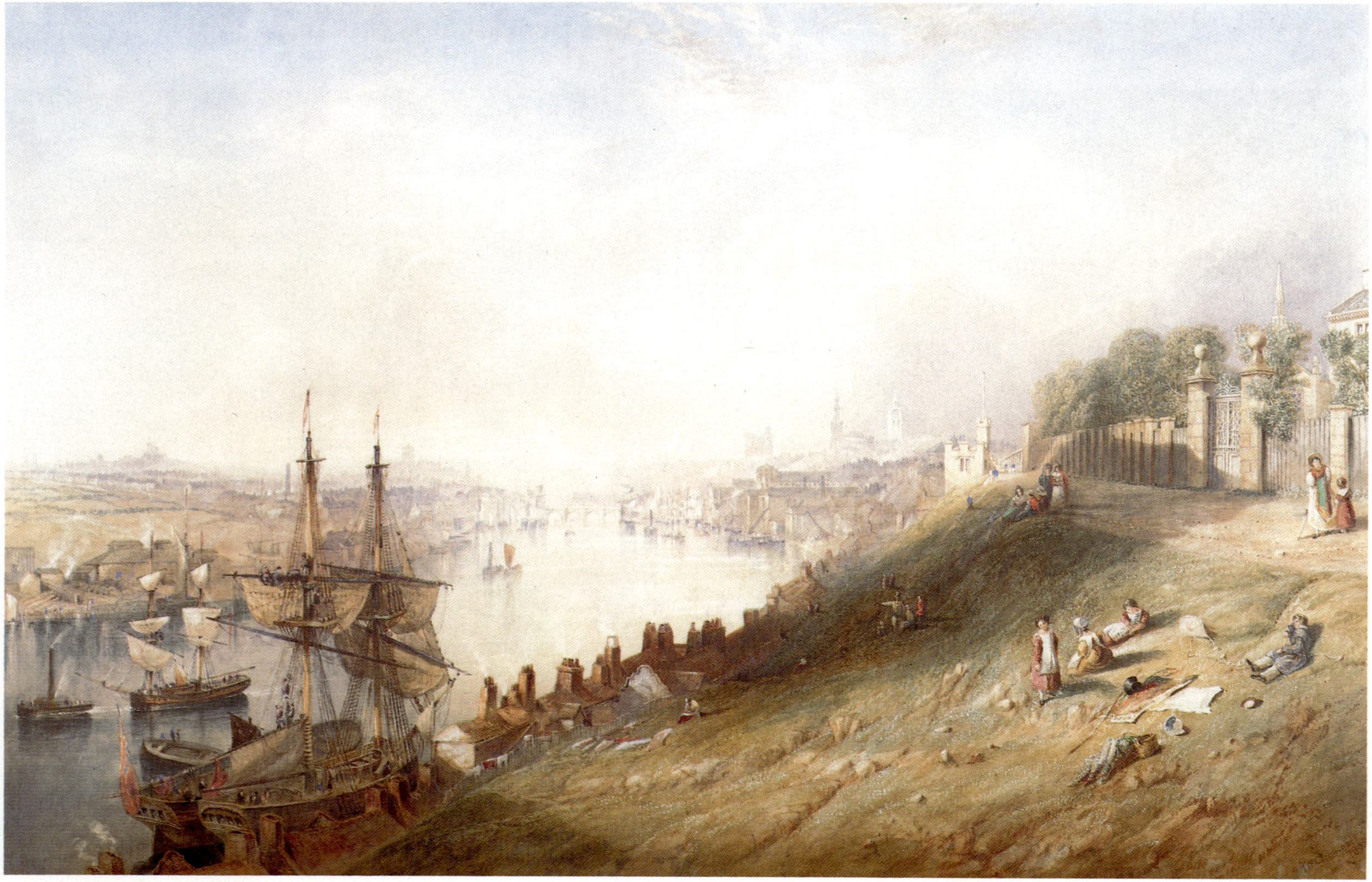

Newcastle from St. Ann's. 1835. *Laing Art Gallery, Newcastle upon Tyne (Tyne and Wear Museum)*

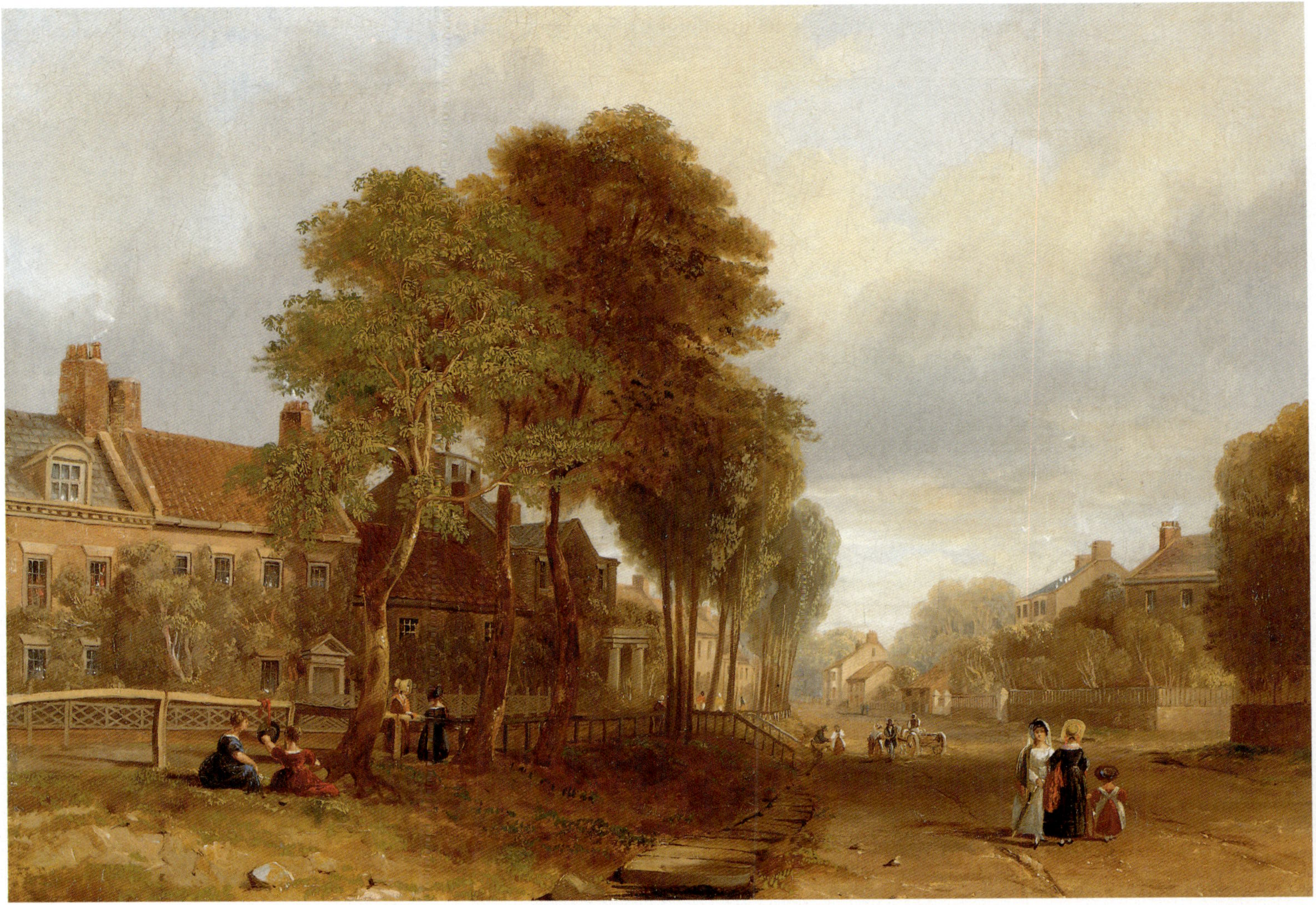

Westoe Village. 1838. *South Shields Art Gallery (Tyne and Wear Museum)*

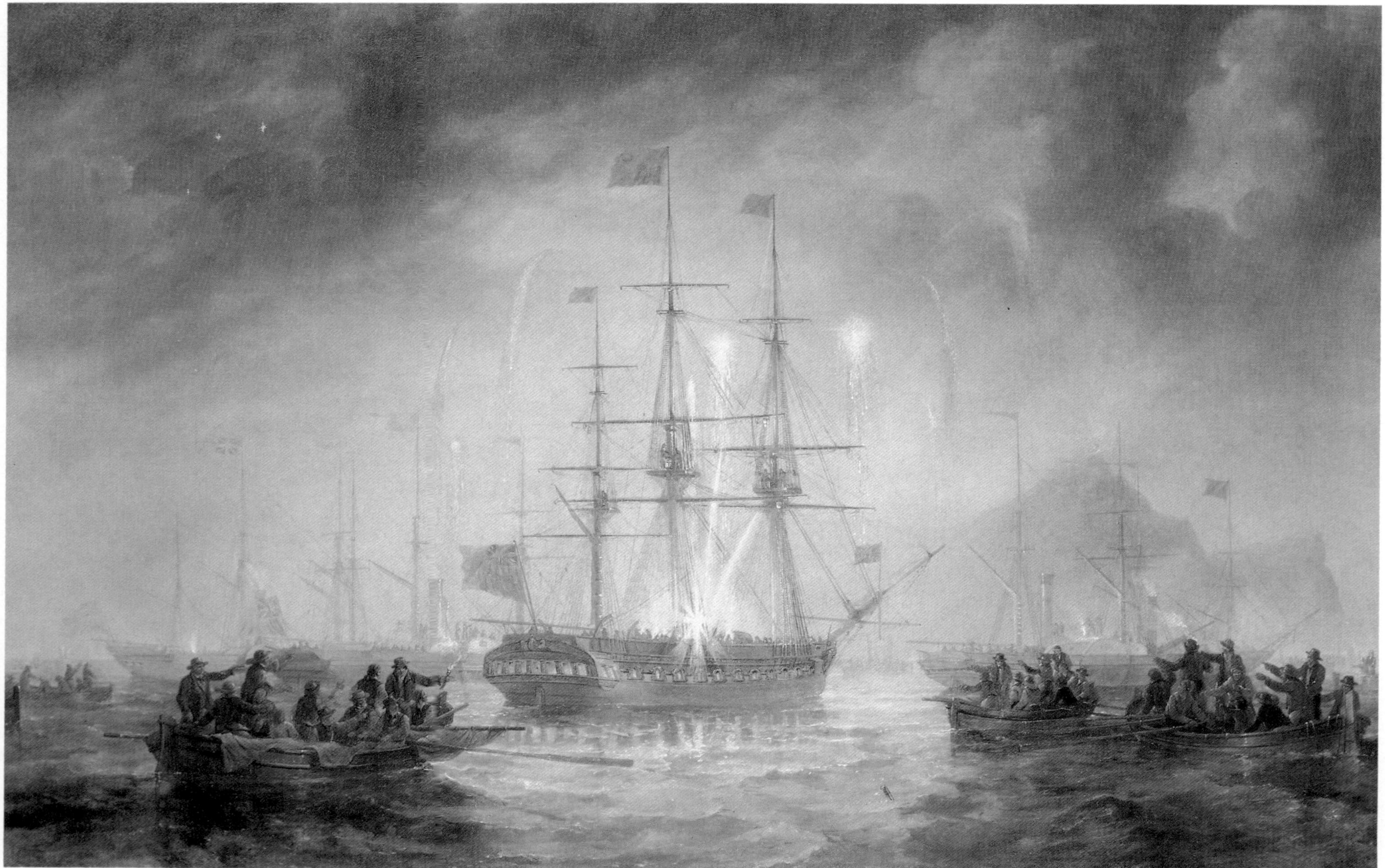

The arrival of HM Queen Victoria with the Royal Squadron off Edinburgh on the night of August 31st 1842. *York City Art Gallery*

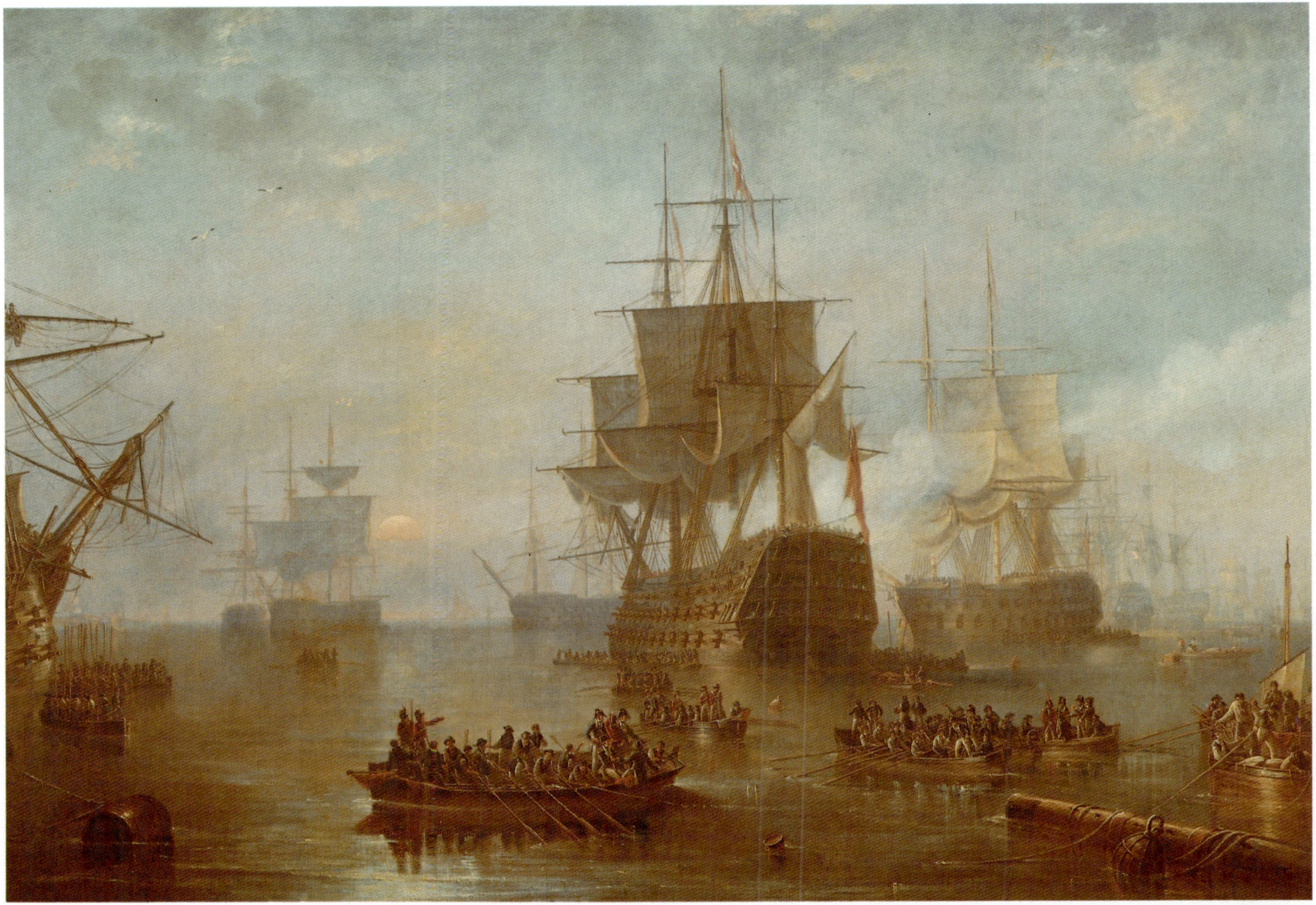

HMS Victory off the Isle of Wight. *Royal Naval Museum, Portsmouth*

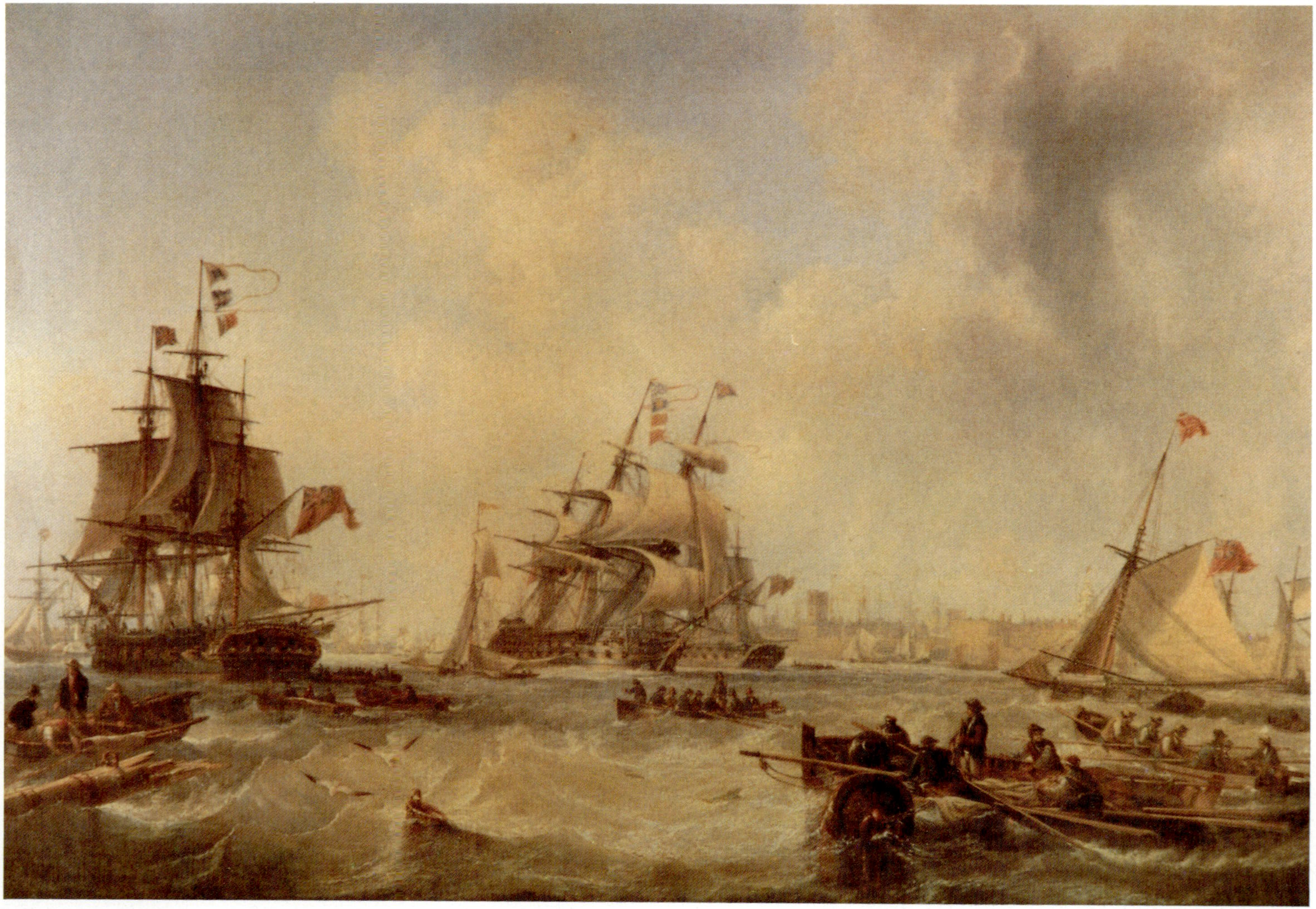

Men-of-War off Portsmouth Harbour. 1848. *Laing Art Gallery, Newcastle upon Tyne (Tyne and Wear Museum)*

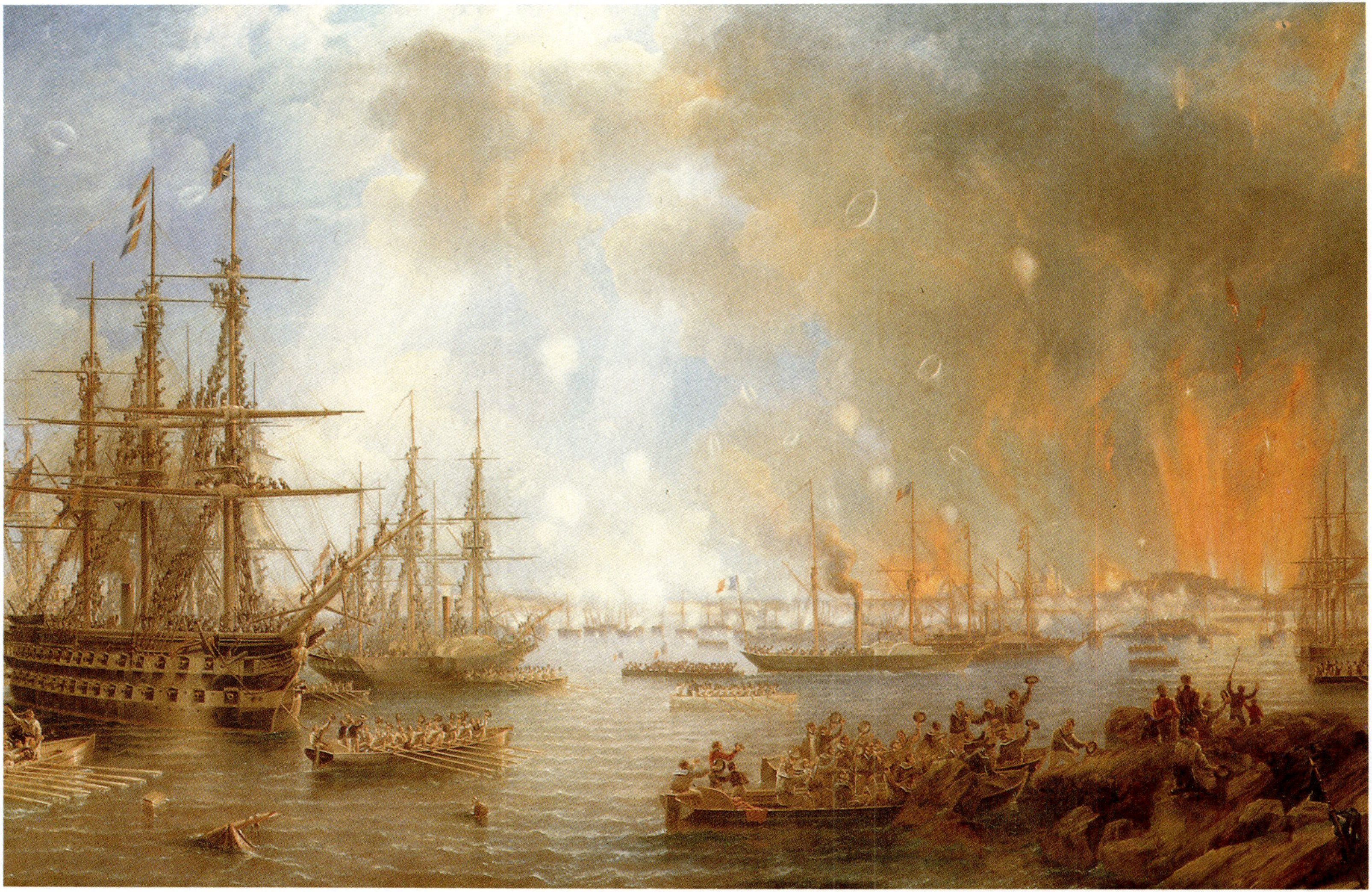

The Bombardment of Sveaborg. 1855. *National Maritime Museum, London*

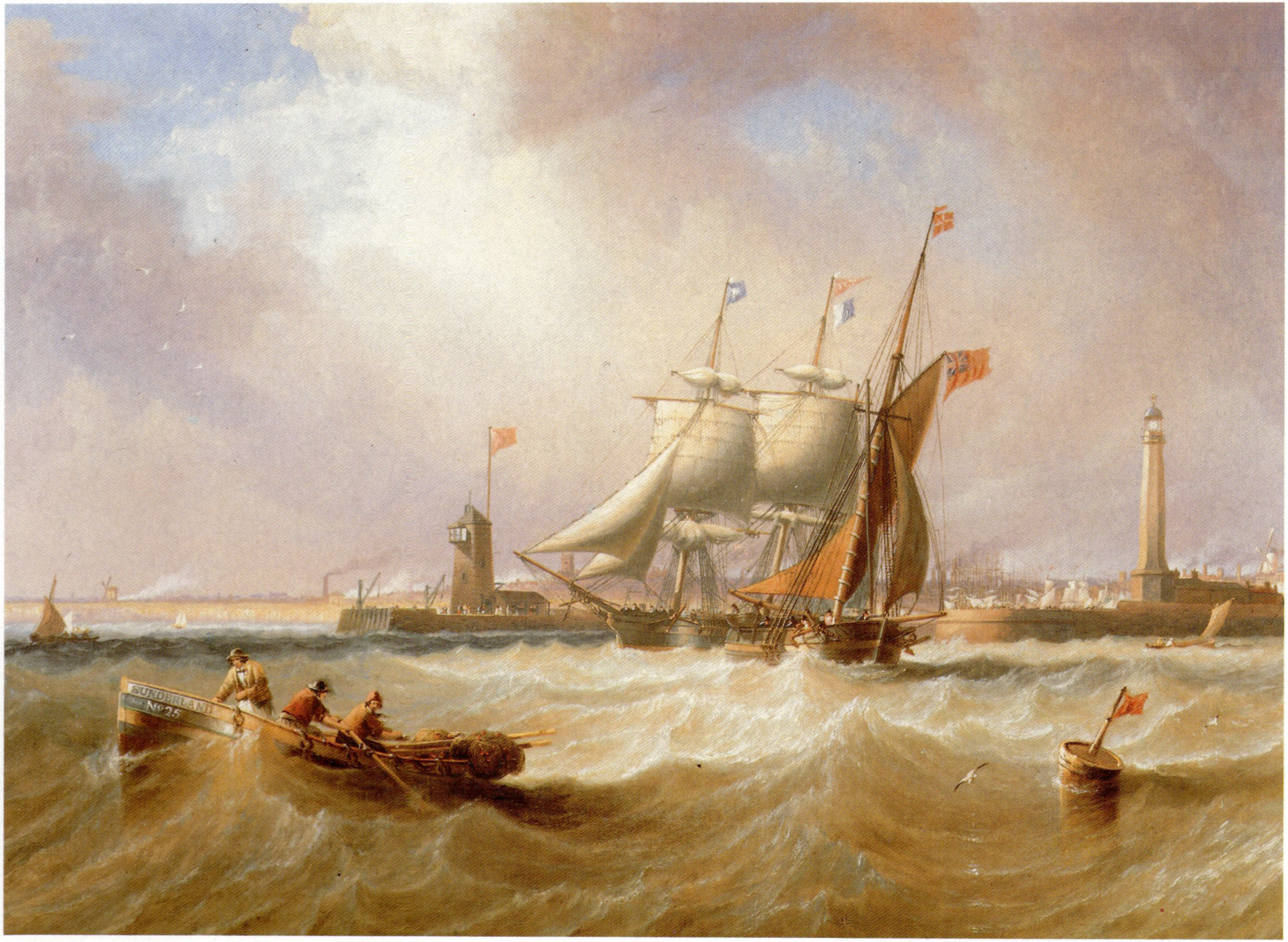

Sunderland Harbour. 1864. *Sunderland Art Gallery (Tyne and Wear Museum)*

Seven

THE FIRST LONDON YEARS

The London in which the Carmichaels arrived was one of change. By 1846 Queen Victoria had reigned for nine years. When she had succeeded to the throne the boundaries of the capital would have roughly been; to the north, half of Regent's Park; then going west to the Edgeware Road the boundary would have run down Park Lane to Hyde Park Corner and on to Westminster Bridge. The river was the southern boundary. This had been the whole of London proper; that is to say not the City of London, nor London with her suburbs of orchards, hamlets, market gardens and then open country.

Bloomsbury was the principal suburb and was where the middle classes tended to live. In the class conscious society of the Victorians, an artist's family

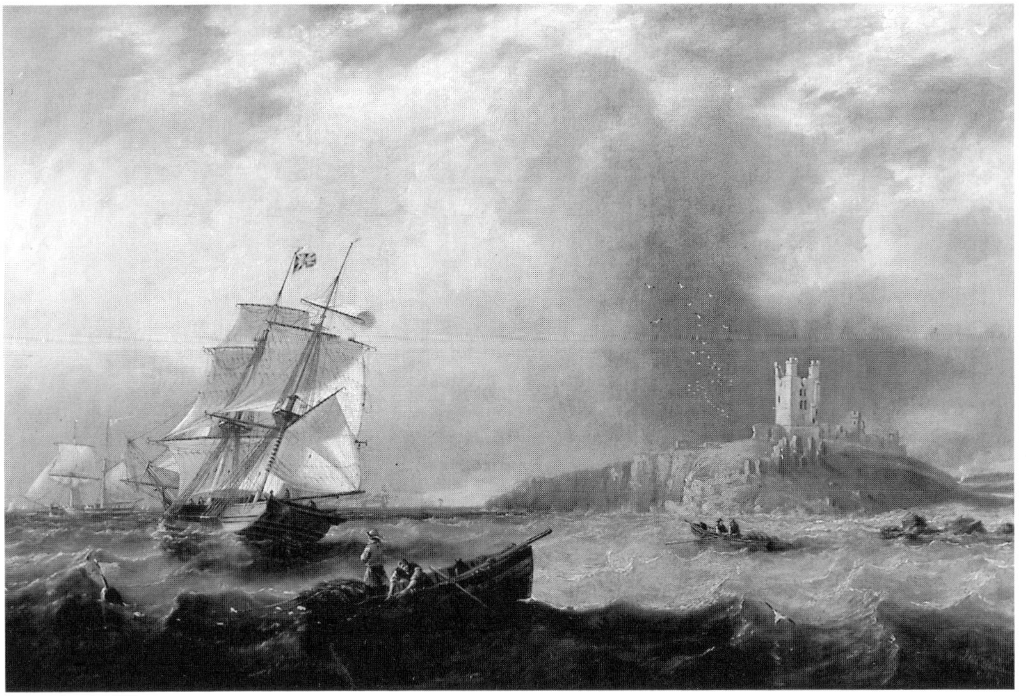

Shipping off Dunstanburgh Castle. 1847. *The Lord Mayor of Newcastle upon Tyne.*
This oil hangs in the Mansion House and was completed
the year after Carmichael moved to London.

would have been documented into the middle class. Bloomsbury contained the British Museum which had been established by an Act of Parliament in 1753, and clustered around this building were Russell and Bedford Squares which were very grand.

The Carmichael's first address was a little west of there, off the broad Tottenham Court Road at number 20 Howland Street. Unfortunately none of the original houses are still standing, but a glance at Tallis's *Street Views of London*[1] shows it to have been a street lined with good four storey family houses (five if you included the basement). The rent for a two year lease of a house of this size would have probably been about £100 a year with the Agent providing some second class furniture and curtaining.

We cannot be certain that the Carmichaels occupied the whole of the house at the start. An artist called George Barnard gave this address when he exhibited at the British Institution in 1842 so maybe others shared it. But we do know that the census for 1851 mentions only the Carmichael family as living there and this includes one house servant, Elizabeth Morel, aged 27 years.

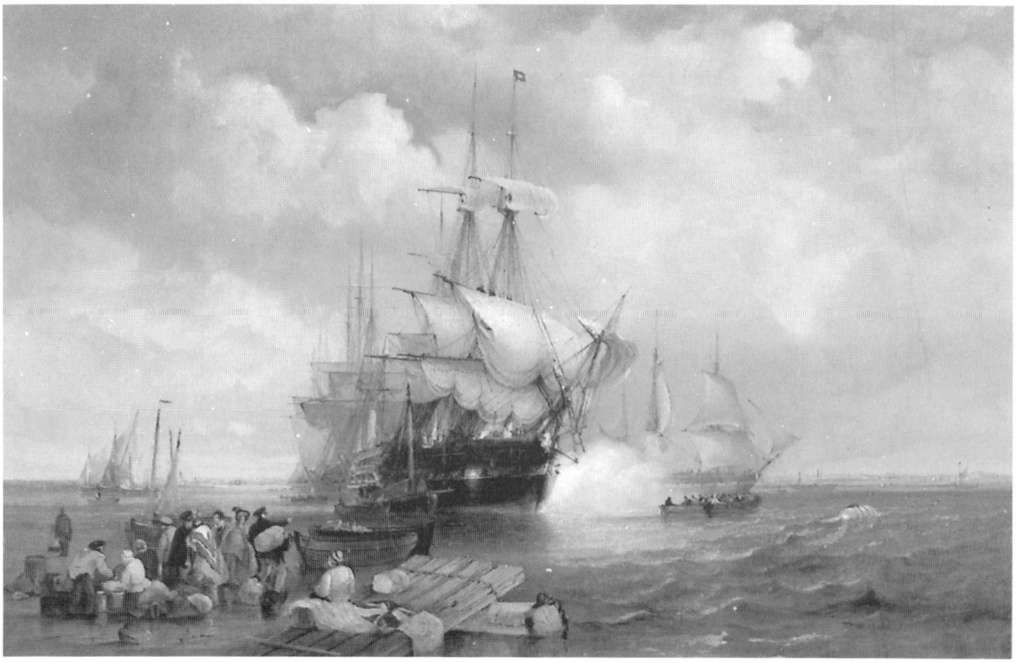

Four Indiamen preparing to leave the lower Thames. *Omell Gallery, London*
Carmichael began to paint more London scenes

It was a good area of London for them to choose for many artists lived or worked around there as we can tell from the addresses of their exhibited works. John Constable[2] when he died in 1837 had had his studio around the corner from Howland Street; George Chambers[3] had lived about a fifteen minutes walk away in Rathbone Place; the new firm of Winsor and Newton had opened nearby in 1832 and soon acquired a reputation for their high quality art materials. With the opening of their chemical works in 1844, they were able to fully justify their advertisement to ..... "gradually improve the quality of all paints to ensure the purity of pigments and perfect preparations for the Artist's palette."

No doubt Carmichael would have missed the proximity of his friend Thomas Carrick[4] who was living some way away in Upper Seymour Street; and two other Newcastle artists were at a distance; Richardson junior[5] was in Hyde Park and Henry Perlee Parker[6] had shut himself off in Hammersmith.

In the 1840s there was much going on for the artists in London. There were art galleries, exhibitions and lectures where they could meet and discuss their work. The National Gallery had come into being in 1824. In 1846 the idea of a National Portrait Gallery was being discussed and was actually founded in 1856. And way back in 1766 James Christie senior had founded the firm of picture auctioneers. There were lecture meetings to go to at the Royal Geographical Society and the Royal Society, and there were winter lectures held by the Royal Academy at Somerset House. However, bearing in mind Carmichael's financial situation it is doubtful if he would have spent much time away from his painting. In those first years in London he certainly had a full schedule of work, though according to Aaron Watson[7] it was not until June 6th 1846 that Carmichael wrote in his journal "Began work in London".

DIFFICULTIES WITH WORK

From several entries in a journal that Watson refers to in his memoir, we gather that for the first year or so after his move Carmichael's work did not go too smoothly. In 1846 he did not show any work at the Royal Academy, the Society of British Artists at Suffolk Street nor at the British Institution. One entry says ..... "After working six days at a sea-piece of the Phantom Ship, I cut it up and put it into the fire", and another says "..... I worked hard all day, whether for better or worse I cannot tell."[8] These remarks seem somewhat immature for a gifted artist but perhaps Carmichael was just feeling depressed or even unwell for we know that he did suffer at times from ill-health. However there do not appear to be any long breaks in his work for illness, though there are the occasional references to his feelings, as at the end of 1851 when he wrote "Thank God I have not been during this year stopped with ill-health or for any other cause."[9]

Many of these feelings were more than likely caused by overwork for he was certainly a prolific painter and at times this must have meant a slip in his standards though not with his bigger paintings. Even his admirer Watson says "It must be confessed, indeed, that he painted too many pictures."

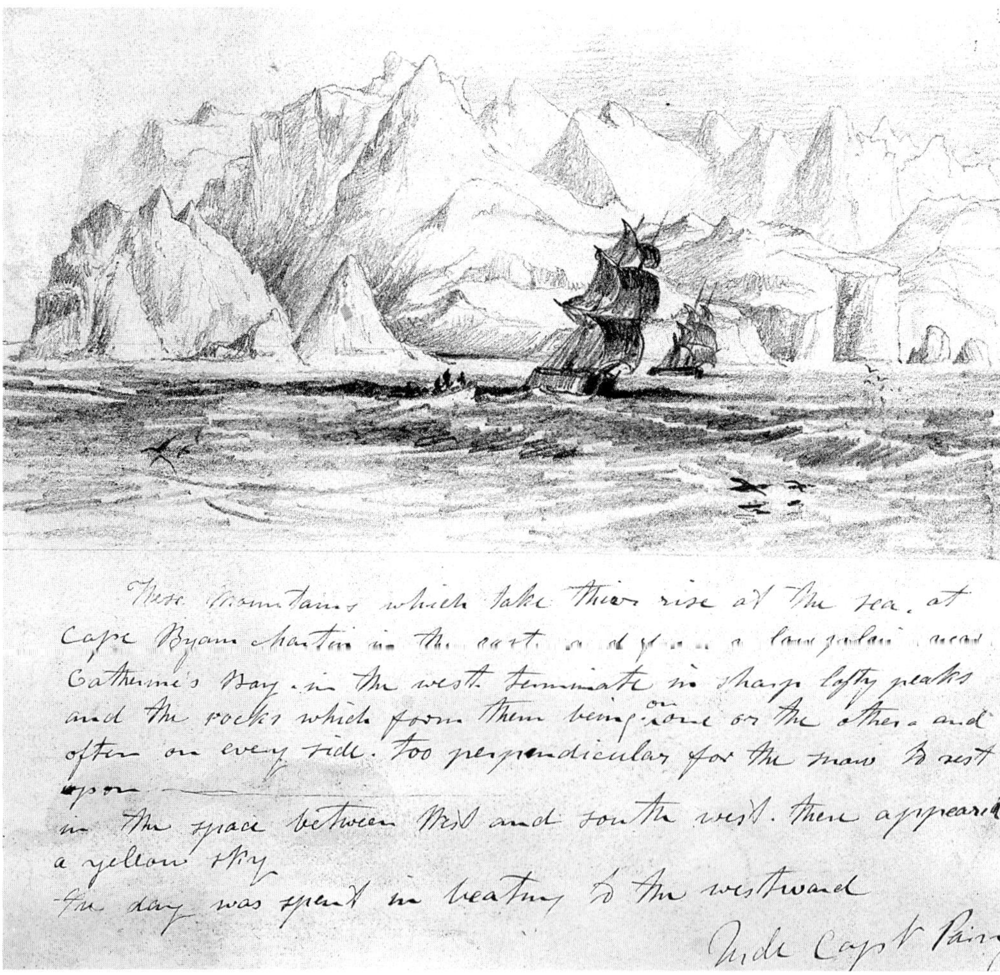

Carmichael completed this mature sketch for a painting from Captain Parry's details of a voyage that he made in 1827. *Private Collection*

But one must bear in mind that Carmichael relied on a high output of smaller seascapes (pot-boilers) to pay his bills, and a number of these may have caused the criticism that he could be an erratic painter.

However by 1847 he had his exhibition pieces ready. One of *Shields Harbour* was exhibited at the British Institution and he sent three to the Society of British Artists. That summer he also showed two pictures at the Royal Academy – *On the Thames at Woolwich* and *The Needles, Isle of Wight with Shipping*. Of the latter the reviewer in *The Art Journal* for 1847 remarked on the artist's treatment of the sea as being "..... painted with much freshness and natural movement" but Carmichael himself was upset as the picture was 'skied' – in other words hung too high to be seen to an advantage and he wrote in his journal "I hope to live long enough to make them treat me better."[10]

In those first months he could also have had fears that he had made the wrong decision in moving to London and perhaps for the first time he met the strict class consciousness of the Victorians, something that would not have been so noticeable in the provinces. In London the middle class knew its place and as we have heard the artists were automatically part of those middle classes together with the poets, novelists, essayists and journalists. 'Society' were a class apart. Men in professions of any kind, except the two Services, could only belong to society by right of birth and family connections. Men in trade, even bankers, were counted as tradesmen and could not possibly qualify.[11] Perhaps Carmichael was aware of this and he missed the friendlier, provincial life where being a good artist was more important than birth. But his sense of humour would have helped him through and he never minded telling stories against himself such as the one he told William Bell Scott,[12] "I couldn't stand the dullness of the social evening – I couldn't stand it – so at last I stood up and danced a hornpipe by myself; but I was soon stopped off, for instead of anybody following my example, they looked at each other as if they thought I had gone mad!" And Watson tells a story of Carmichael – "He always preserved his Northern habit of speech, and had so much difficulty in making himself understood in London society that on one occasion a lady asked him how long he had lived in England and wondered that he had not made more progress with the language!"

So it seems that Carmichael's natural good spirits did not allow him to remain depressed for too long and his determination soon conquered any disappointments. By the end of 1847 he had completed several major works. The first was a theme that interested him most of his life – the adventures of the British explorer, Sir John Franklin, in the Polar Seas – and he did several sketches of Franklin's second voyage in 1826 and one of Franklin's fellow explorer, Captain William Parry's, voyage in 1827. They are mature sketches done from details brought back by the two. Carmichael retained a fascination for Franklin's voyage and the mystery of his final disappearance, and perhaps it was Parry who obtained him a commission to paint the pictures of the two ships *The Erebus and the Terror.*

These two vessels had first come to the notice of the public in 1839 when the Royal Society had urged the Government to send an expedition to the Antarctic to study the earth's magnetic field in an attempt to locate the southern magnetic pole. Accordingly the *Erebus*, 370 tons, and the *Terror,* 340 tons, under the command of Sir James Clark Ross, were fitted out for the Antarctic waters. Six

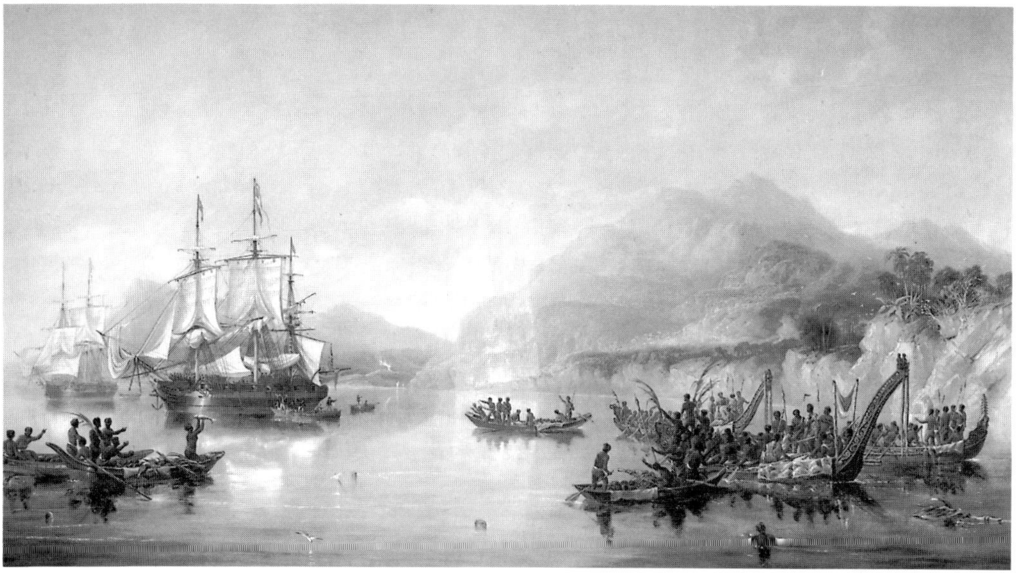

Erebus and Terror at anchor off New Zealand. 1847.
National Maritime Museum, Greenwich

years later in May 1845 these same ships set out on another expedition, this time under the command of Sir John Franklin. They set off to look for the north-west passage to the Pacific, but things went wrong and nothing more was heard. (An expedition organised in 1993 found two of Franklin's men but there was no sign of where Franklin himself is buried and exactly what caused their deaths. A recently discovered log book records his death as June 11th 1847).

Carmichael was commissioned to paint two contrasting views of the first expedition. One picture shows the two vessels cutting through the ice off the newly discovered Victoria Island and the other, shown here, is of them lying peacefully at anchor off the Bay of Islands in New Zealand – perhaps in this painting Carmichael has allowed himself to stray a little over the limit of 'an artist's licence'. The countryside is shown as mountainous and densely palmed whereas the Bay of Islands is undulating and under 1,200 feet and has few trees. Furthermore the ships differ slightly in the two pictures, and the Maori canoes in the foreground of the one are not accurate. This is a most unusual slip for Carmichael to make. One wonders if he was still feeling unsettled with his new life? However this particular picture has some historical artistic interest as it is one of the few large scale oil paintings produced in the first half of the 19th century that includes Maori figures.[13]

As mentioned Carmichael was fascinated with the stories surrounding Sir John Franklin's disappearance and a painting that he did for the 1850 Royal Academy exhibition was of one of the many official and private searches.[14] No fewer than fifteen ships were directly or indirectly engaged over the years in the search to try and solve the mystery of what happened to Franklin, his 129 companions and the two ships. Carmichael called his painting *Voyagers in the cause of humanity – Commander Collingwood and Captain McLure in search of Sir John Franklin.* It brought praise from the reviewer in *The Art Journal* that year when he wrote – "These two ships hold on their course obliquely into the picture, sailing under easy canvas in each other's wake ..... The painting of the water and the drawing of the vessels, manifest extensive knowledge in this department of art."

SETTLED AT LAST IN LONDON

Few criticisms can have been passed about Carmichael's next two pictures of *HMS Victory,* both painted in the 1840s and about the same size. The first, *Lord Nelson's Victory at Trafalgar – Close of Battle* and the second, *HMS Victory off the Isle of Wight.* It was not the first time that he had painted this famous ship though he had been only 6 years old when the Battle of Trafalgar had taken place.

In choosing the *Victory*, Carmichael was following or pre-empting many painters of his day; Turner[16] had painted *Victory* and, back in 1806, Constable had exhibited at the Academy a much acclaimed painting of the ship. Thomas

Butterworth,[17] Nicholas Pocock,[18] Samuel Drummond,[19] Charles Stanfield[20] and many others had, since 1805, been painting scenes showing the *Victory* before, during and after the Battle of Trafalgar.

In the second contrasting view, *HMS Victory* is lying off St. Helens in the Isle of Wight. On board is the body of Vice Admiral Lord Nelson awaiting burial until the preparations for the State funeral have been completed. Around the *Victory* other ships are anchored. All is still; it is probably sunset. To give interest to the sky Carmichael has painted in some threatening clouds, with a build up of blues, greys and yellows, but they are not as yet enough to affect the movement of the water where the reflections lie bright and motionless. The

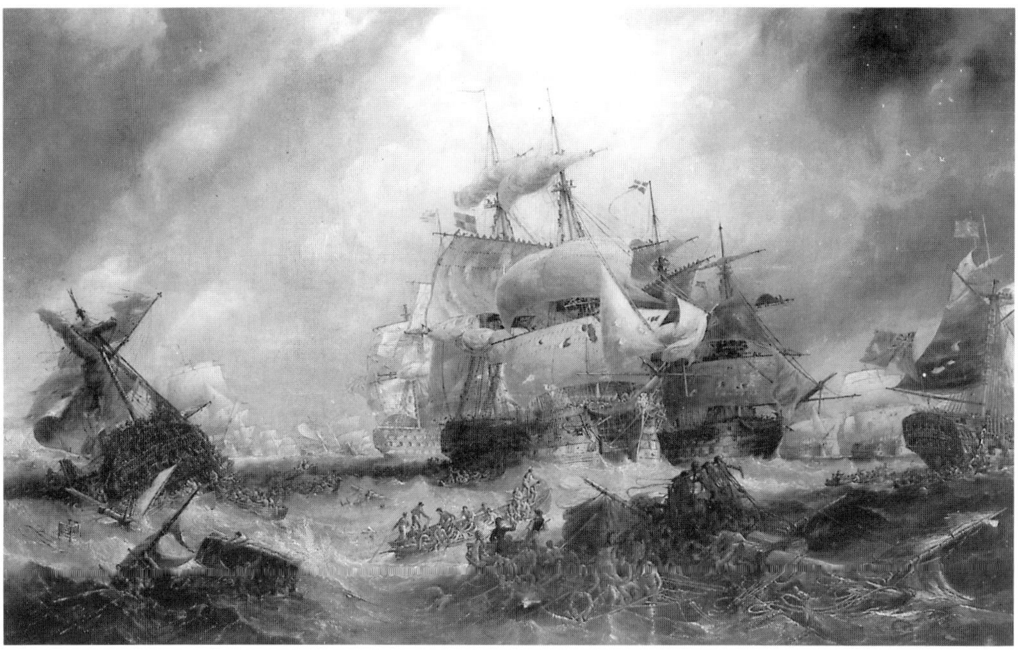

Lord Nelson's Victory at Trafalgar. Close of Battle. *Sotheby's, London*

whole picture reminds one of a Canaletto. Has Carmichael gone right back to his early days for his inspiration of this scene, to those first Canalettos he saw at the Northern Academy in Newcastle? In the forefront he has painted several longboats crowded with sailors and here, bearing in mind Carmichael's hesitancy in drawing faces, one begins to wonder if once again he has collaborated with a fellow artist for every sailor has a distinctive face. If someone else did do them, that was all he was allowed to do; the whole composition is typically Carmichael and can be listed among his finest work. It hangs in the Royal Naval Museum in Portsmouth Dockyard and is to be seen on posters, gallery guides and greeting cards and a few years ago it went on show in Japan.

A picture of this size, approximately 55" x 80", must have been a commission. There is no record of it having ever been exhibited but it would certainly have been acclaimed at the time, as was the painting *Heavy weather; riding on a lee shore* which he exhibited at the Royal Academy in 1849 and which brought praise from *The Art Journal* reviewers when they said "the description is very circumstantial insomuch as we are all anxiety for her fate. We pray that she may hold her own till the turn of the tide. The sea-pieces of this artist are always admirable, because always true, no living painter more happily combines portraiture (in shipping) with the picturesque."[21]

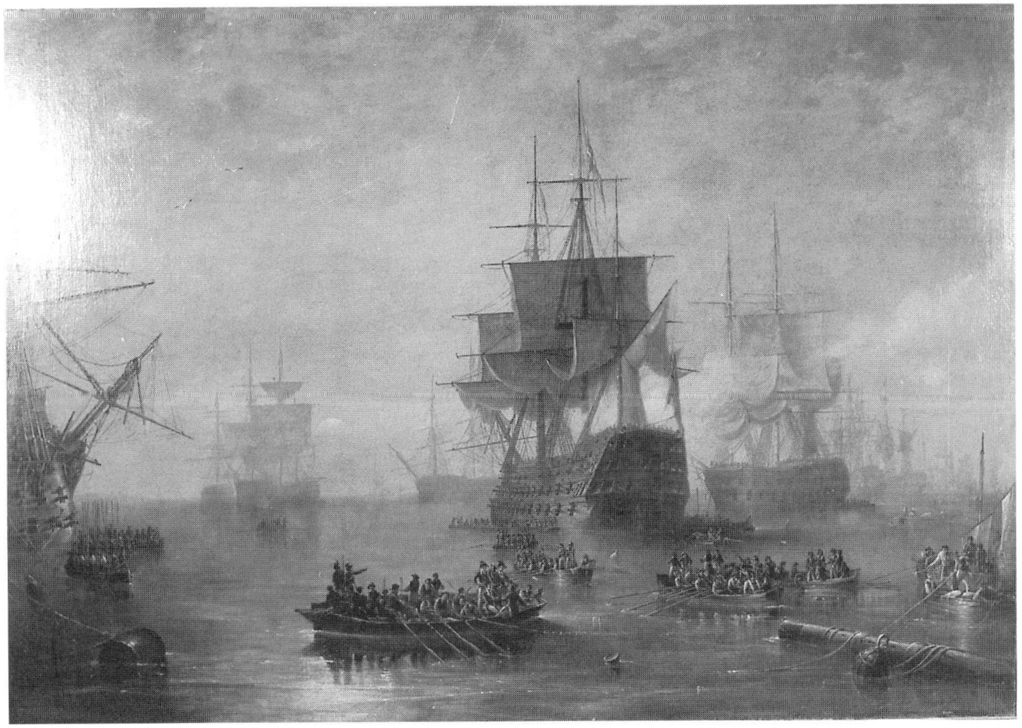

HMS Victory off the Isle of Wight.
Royal Naval Museum, Portsmouth
(see colour plates)

We gather from those words that Carmichael was now becoming as well known in London as the provinces. But for a man nearing fifty we know that he set himself a punishing schedule and there were always money worries. For this reason he must have been relieved when their eldest daughter Margaret got married.

Frederick William Gustave Schmalz was around the age of thirty when he married Margaret Carmichael; she was twenty four. Born in Germany, Gustave had been an orphan for many years before he started work as Secretary to the British Consul in Dantzig. After five years the young man left and went to live in Newcastle where he started a business, and was introduced into the Carmichael family. He and Margaret were married at St. Pancras Church in London on 1st May 1850. The witnesses were a John Lee and Margaret Jane, who Carmichael described as being "daughter of my kind friend Mr. Dobson." Margaret had made a good marriage. She travelled with Gustave on business; he became Prussian Consul in Newcastle; and their daughter, Maria Flora, was born in 1851. Later they built themselves a house out in Ryton and Carmichael painted them a picture to go over the fireplace of their new home; it was an Arctic scene and another search for Sir John Franklin, this time with the *Enterprise and the Investigator.*

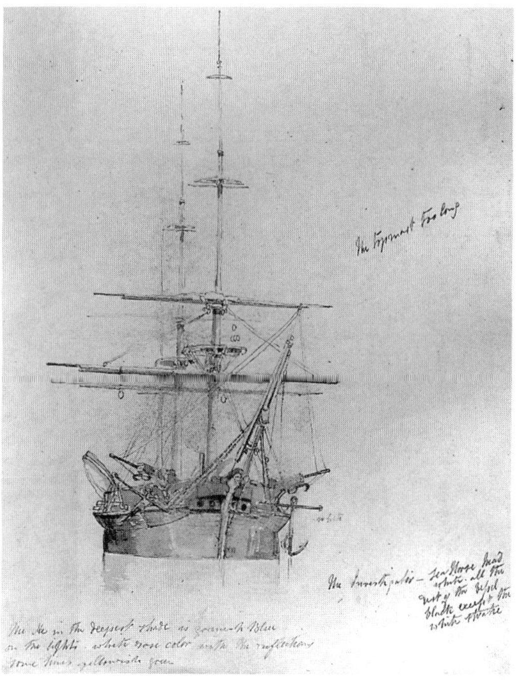

The Investigator.
Laing Art Gallery, Newcastle upon Tyne (Tyne and Wear Museum)

We are told in a book by Trevor Blakemore[22] that the picture was extremely realistic. He writes – "Among the icebergs a great wind sprang up suddenly, throwing the two boats completely out of control, in which state they had to run the gauntlet of five mountains of moving ice; yet they remained miraculously uninjured." Admiral Collinson was in command of this particular expedition and appears to have been a friend of Carmichael and accompanied the artist down to Woolwich so he could sketch the actual ships and get the correct details. Unfortunately although the picture was "much prized by the whole family" it has disappeared, but we do have this sketch that Carmichael did of the *Investigator.*

Aaron Watson[23] tells us that it is questionable whether Carmichael "strengthened his art by his removal to London, although the wider sphere of work undoubtedly extended his fame. In Newcastle he had been subjected to no strong influences ..... He had worked without that restraint which comes of seeing too much of the work and feeling too strongly the rivalry of others." Certainly during his time in London his work was varied as he kept up with the subjects and scenes that many marine artists were chasing.

Naturally the shipping off the busy ports and dockyards like Chatham, Portsmouth and Plymouth drew the artists. Nicholas Pocock did scenes off Portsmouth; so did Anthony Copling Fielding,[24] the Joy brothers,[25] John and William actually lived there; and Henry Luscombe[26] recorded varied aspects of maritime life off the south coast. Among them Carmichael painted *Portsmouth Harbour* and *Men of War off Portsmouth* (see colour plates).

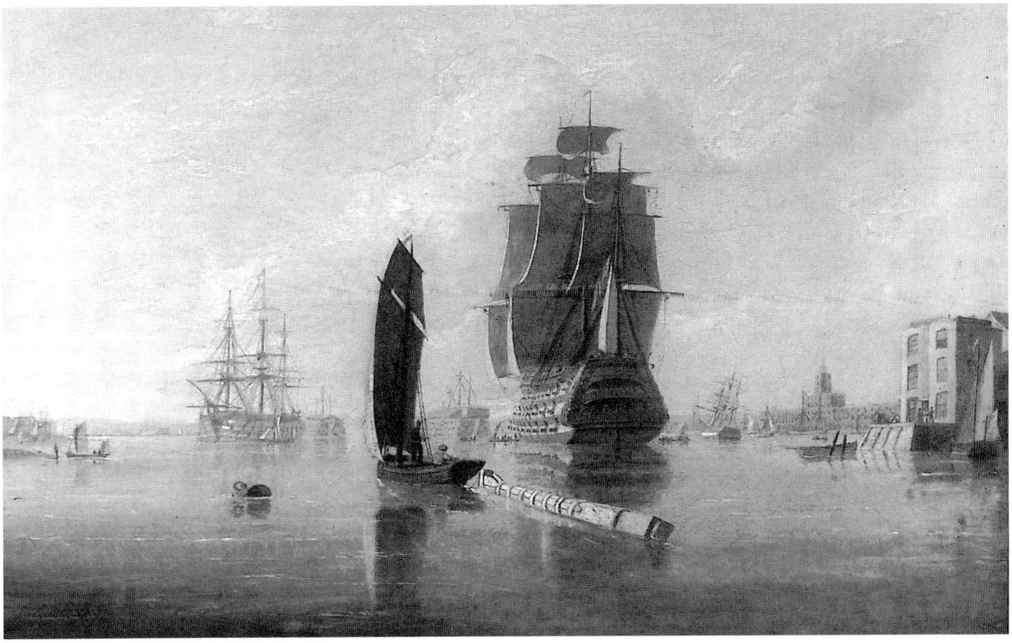

Portsmouth Harbour. *Christies Images, London*

From Portsmouth harbour the artist could take a steam packet via Ryde to Cowes in the Isle of Wight which became especially interesting when, in 1845, the Royal Family started to use Osborne House as their summer retreat.

By the second decade of the 1800s the British were emigrating to the seaside during the summer months; a doctor in Brighton had discovered that sea bathing was good for everyone so that resort in particular became popular. With the building of the Chain Pier in 1823, Constable was in Brighton to paint it three years later, and Turner followed in 1828 to name two of the more famous names. Carmichael did several views of the resort – in 1847 *The Seafront and Brighton with fishermen and their boats on the beach* and in the Brighton Art Gallery there is his *Kemp Town from the Sea*. Here, because they were a comparative novelty, Carmichael shows the bathing machines, complete with modesty hoods, and in the foreground is his usual pattern of seagulls and the floating spar. The people are also too far away to have faces and some are wearing the 'Carmichael' red woollen caps.

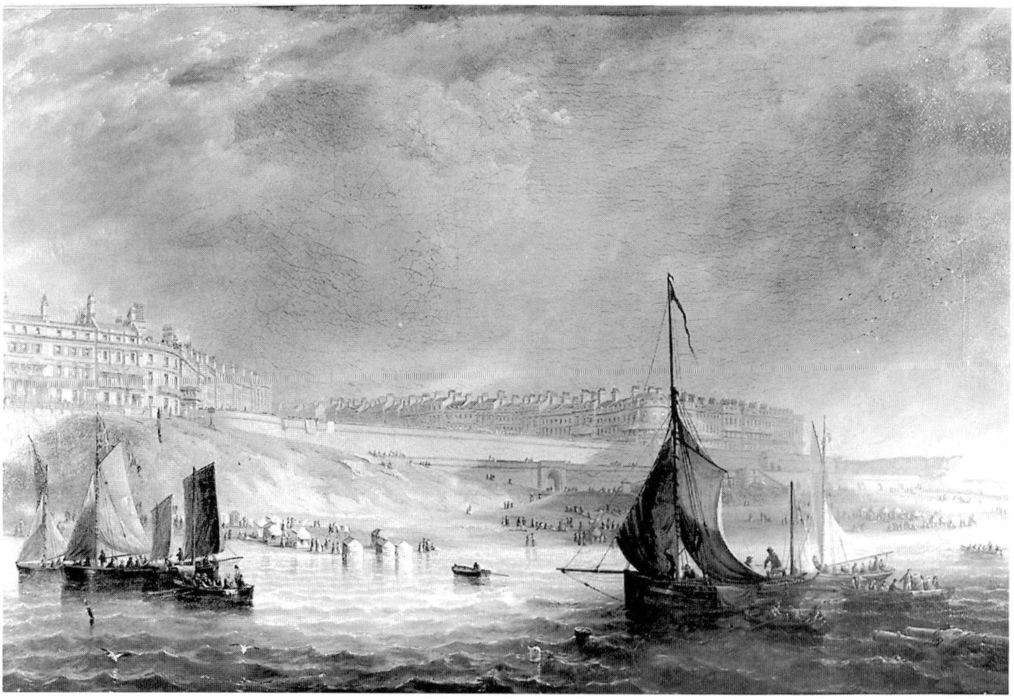

Kemp Town from the sea, Brighton.

Royal Pavilion Art Gallery and Museums, Brighton

Here, because bathing machines were a new idea, Carmichael took care to show them

He probably also enjoyed his journeys down to get his pictures. The train journey from London Bridge station to Brighton took 2 hours and fifty five minutes and on occasions Carmichael must have stopped off on the way, for in 1848 he exhibited two 'railway' pictures at the Royal Academy. These are described as being "designed by, and from the collection of J.V. Rastrick Esq. C.E., F.R.S." One was *The Ouse Viaduct, on the London and Brighton Railway* and the other *The Brighton Viaduct, on the Brighton Lewes and Hastings Railway.* The former painting received no mention that year in *The Art Journal* but the latter had a fairly grudging sentence "This is rather more an engineering water colour subject, than suitable for an oil picture; it is however as agreeably painted as the material will admit." Here was Carmichael doing some of his "more various in character work" to which Aaron Watson had referred, but we still see signs of some of his own favourite scenes. Scarborough keeps appearing with *Scarborough from the Westward* exhibited at the British Institution in 1849 and again there in 1852 with *Securing wreck north of Scarborough Castle.*

Small fishing villages to bustling ports were all painted. In 1811 Turner had been commissioned to do forty drawings under the title *Views of the Southern Coast of England* – with two hundred pencil sketches he took in all the coast from Margate to Lands End. In 1836 Balmer had started a publication entitled *Ports and Harbours of Great Britain.* Over the years, Carmichael too worked his way along the south coast. Sightings of these keep appearing around the world such as *A View of Rochester* dated 1858 which is in a private collection in California. Many of these artists views tend to concentrate on the shipping with a somewhat vague piece of land. Carmichael cannot be particularly accused of this, so it was perhaps unkind of C.E. Hughes[27] when he singled out Carmichael as "less successful at the water's edge than when he is out at sea and only a vague distance of land is visible".

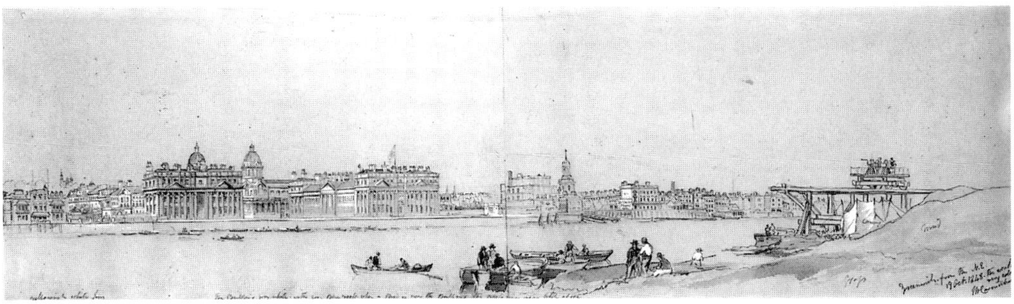

Greenwich from the North East. *National Maritime Museum, London*

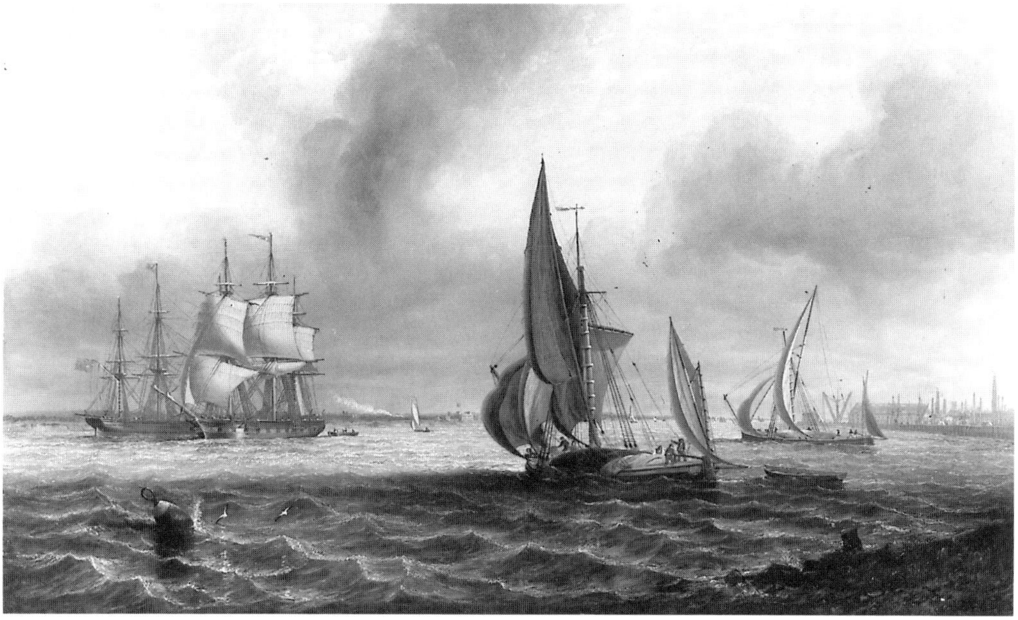

Shipping on the Thames at Woolwich. 1859. *Omell Gallery, London*

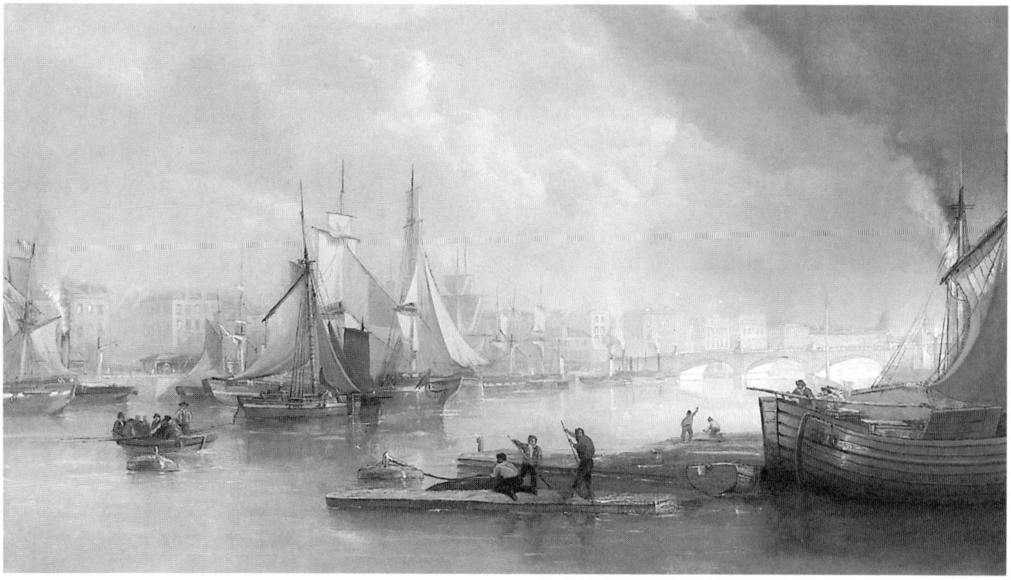

London Bridge. *Omell Gallery, London*

SHIP PORTRAITS

Some of Carmichael's marine work can be classed as ship portraits. This type of painting would be commissioned by the sea Captains or the owners of the Shipping Companies to hang on their boardroom walls. For these the artist would refer to his collections of sketches or copy direct from a ship's model or the ship itself. In this picture of a *Clipper and an East Indiaman leaving Port* we have a ship correct in every detail, but with 'floating objects' and a boat in the forefront, it has a more natural setting. Another painting two years later, *A Clipper and an East Indiaman arriving Home*, also in the Shipley Art Gallery, would appear to be a pair to this.

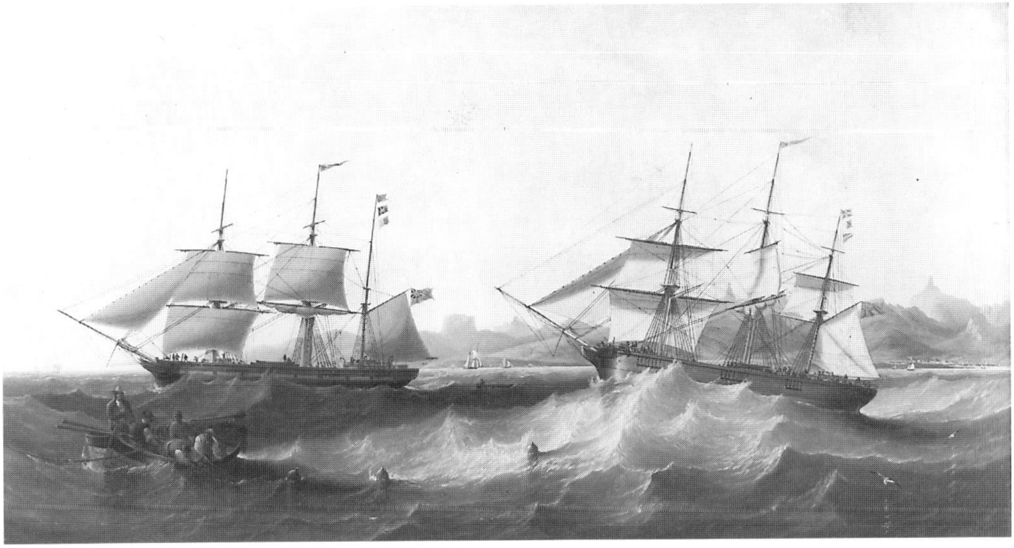

A Clipper and an East Indiaman leaving Port. 1854.
Shipley Art Gallery, Gateshead (Tyne and Wear Museum)

As Aaron Watson says "Carmichael invented a new style. He made the portrait of his ship as correct as even the most exigent Captain could require, but he made it a picture as well." This was difficult to achieve when the primary object was the ship itself and Carmichael tended to call attention to these by giving them a highly polished and luminous look that could have so easily produced a stiff, artificial picture, but this was balanced by the sensitive use he made of colour with his seas and skies. Samuel Walters,[28] William Huggins,[29] Thomas Whitcombe,[30] and others also used a variation of these skills to paint their ship portraits.

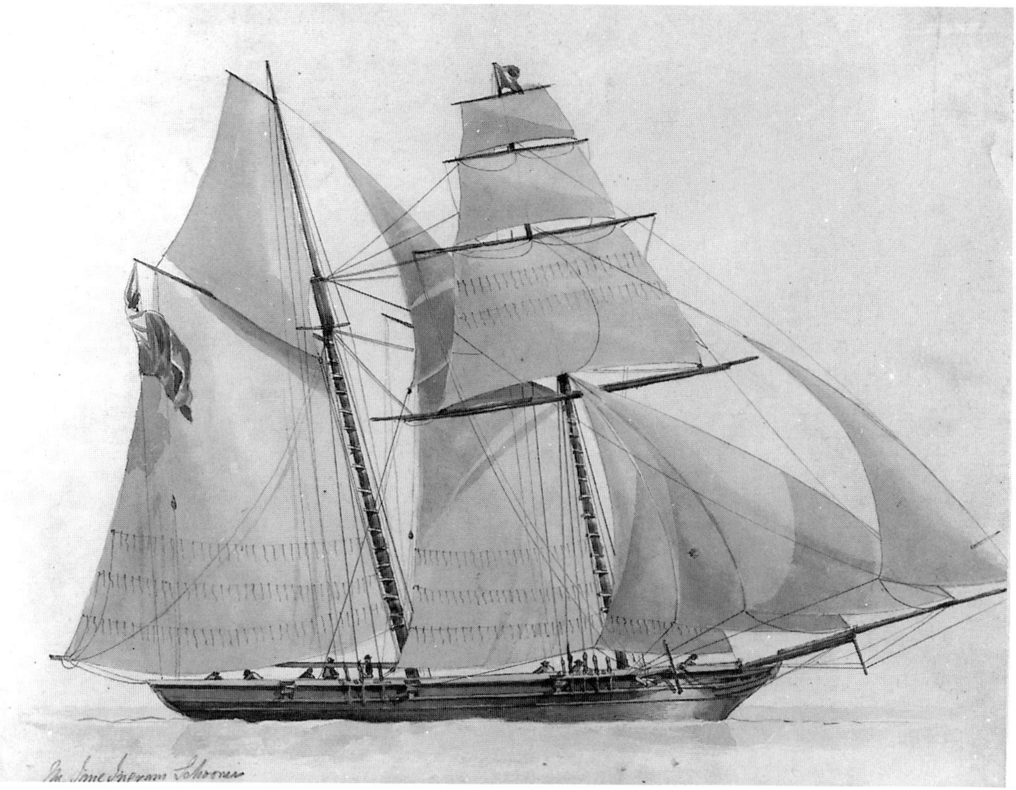

The Jane Ingram Schooner.

Laing Art Gallery, Newcastle upon Tyne (Tyne and Wear Museum)

When the artists in the south were tired of drawing views of the coast there was always the river Thames. Maybe the *Times* of the day was right when they quoted that "the Thames was a cesspool with a tide in it" but it had a lot to offer the artist. Carmichael has left us pictures from all along the course of the river; *Shipping off Sheerness*; *Shipping on the Thames at Woolwich*; *Greenwich from the north-east*; *London Bridge* (see previous pages); *Whitehall Gardens*; *Below Waterloo Bridge*; *Evening scene in the Pool of London*; *Cheyne Walk, from Battersea* and in 1854 he went to Woolwich to draw the *Launch of the Royal Albert* (see page 72).

There was also a lot of building on the river banks for the artists to follow. In 1848 Waterloo station was nearing completion; in 1838 the Houses of Parliament burnt down. Turner painted this and later Carmichael chose the unusual scene *The Houses of Parliament in the Course of Erection*; the building of this part by Sir James Barry's Westminster Palace was finally completed in 1860.

Carmichael still remained in touch with his old life in the north and in 1850 he travelled to Sunderland for the opening of a new dock. Doubtless this would have been a commission from his Patron, Mr. George Hudson MP.

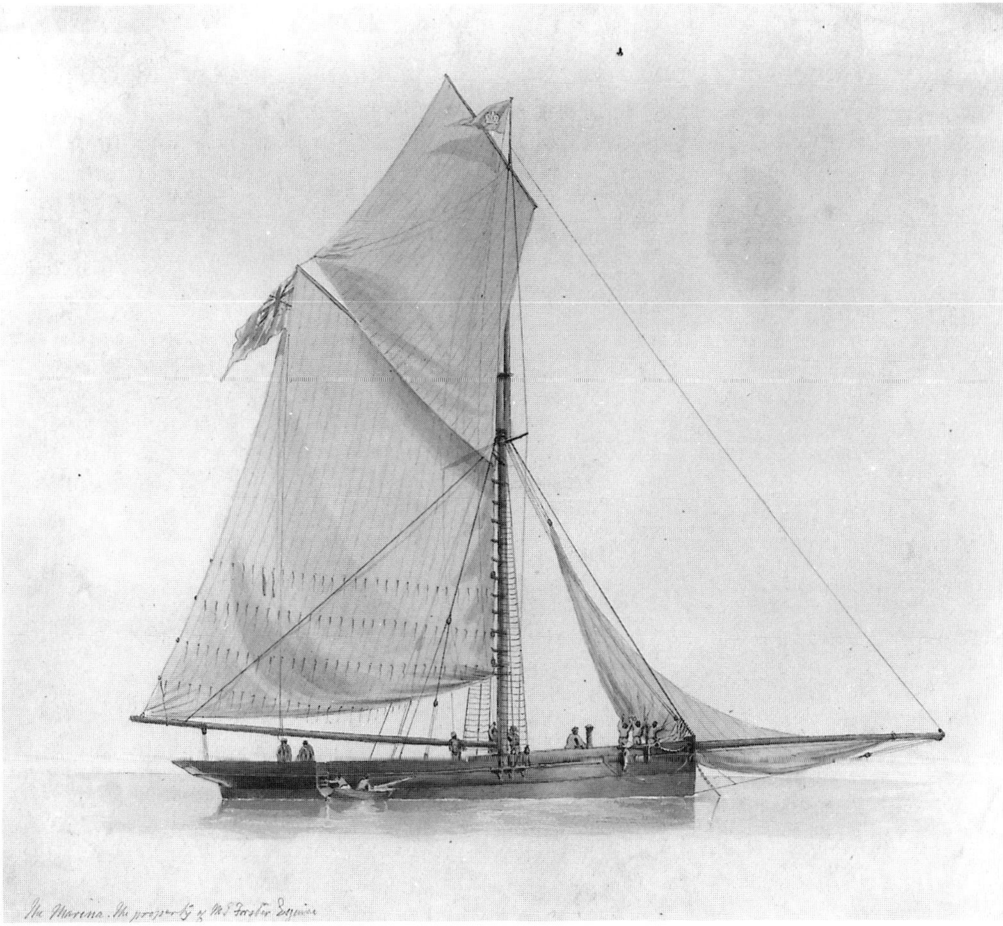

The Marina.

Laing Art Gallery, Newcastle upon Tyne (Tyne and Wear Museum)

These ship studies by Carmichael are two of many in the Laing Art Gallery

So during those first years in London, Carmichael did indeed spread his art widely, but always preferring to do his sea and coastal scenes. Two pictures, done within four years of each other, show clearly how skilled he had become in portraying large and small vessels in choppy or calm conditions.

In *Merchant Shipping* there are at least ten ships all placed in the water at the correct angle. The perspective is excellent; the colour of the sea and sky blend so completely there is no hint as to where one ends and the other begins; and with so many white sails, how right to bring in one of the principal ships with a brown set – you can hear the wind in those sails and the rush of water against the hulls. It is very probable that this picture was one he exhibited at the Royal Academy in 1854 under the title of *Merchant Service*. *The Art Journal*[31] says that "..... among all the nautical pictures of our time, we have never seen vessels so well set in the water." In contrast in the other picture of the *Brayford Pool and Lincoln Cathedral* you can 'hear' the stillness. The detailed rigging on

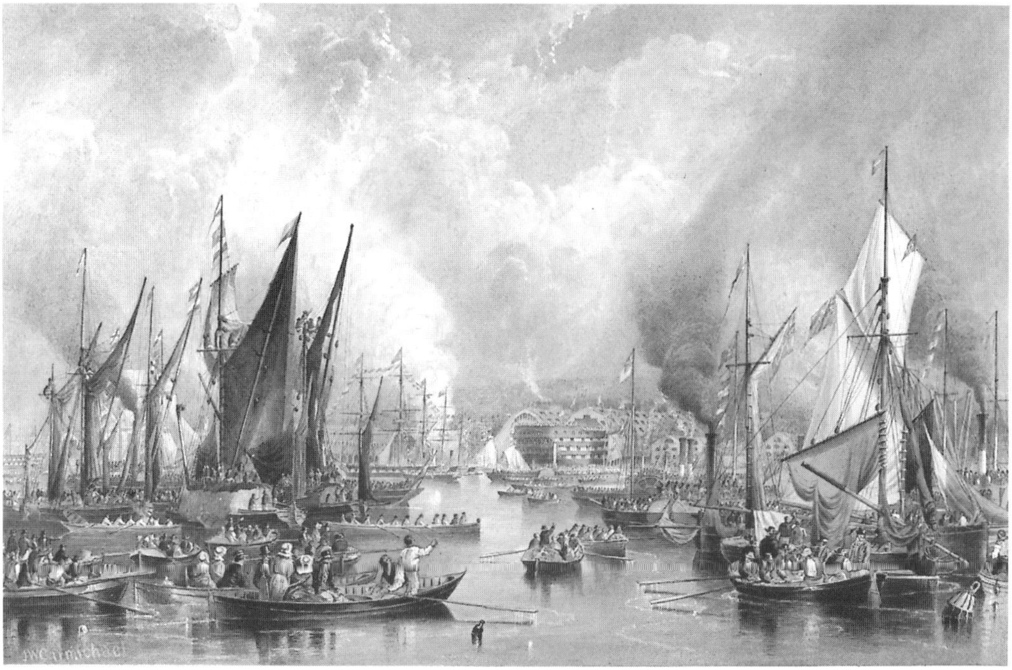

Launch of the Royal Albert. 13th May 1854
The Royal Collection 1994. Her Majesty the Queen

the fishing boats is perfect; their straight masts draw the eye right up to the cathedral; and again there is no definite horizon as the building is absorbed gently into the sky.

These two pictures dispel any doubts that Carmichael's skills had diminished in coming to London. Any smaller slightly more sub-standard sea-pieces that

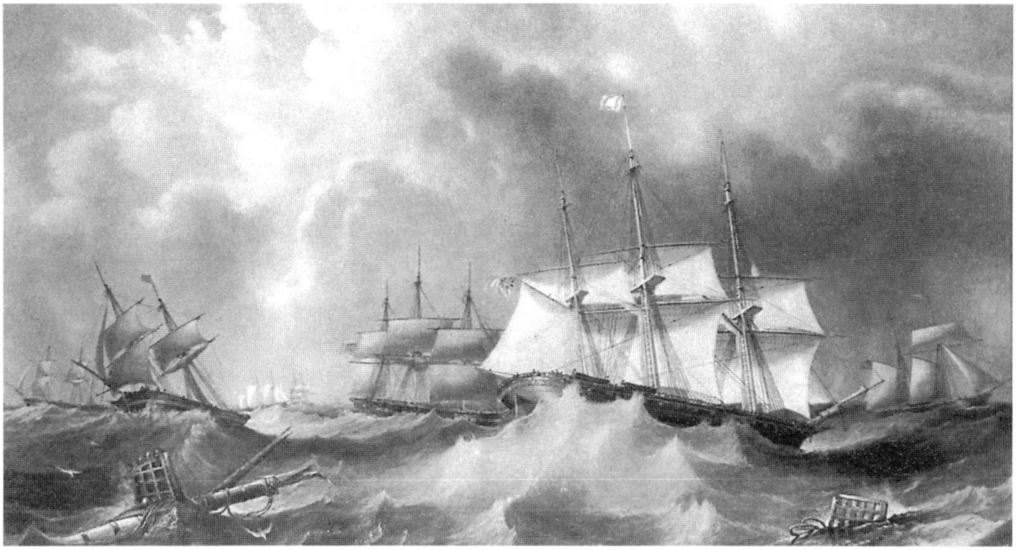

Merchant Shipping. *Gomshall Art Gallery, Guildford*
This was probably exhibited at the Royal Academy in 1854 under the title of 'Merchant Service'

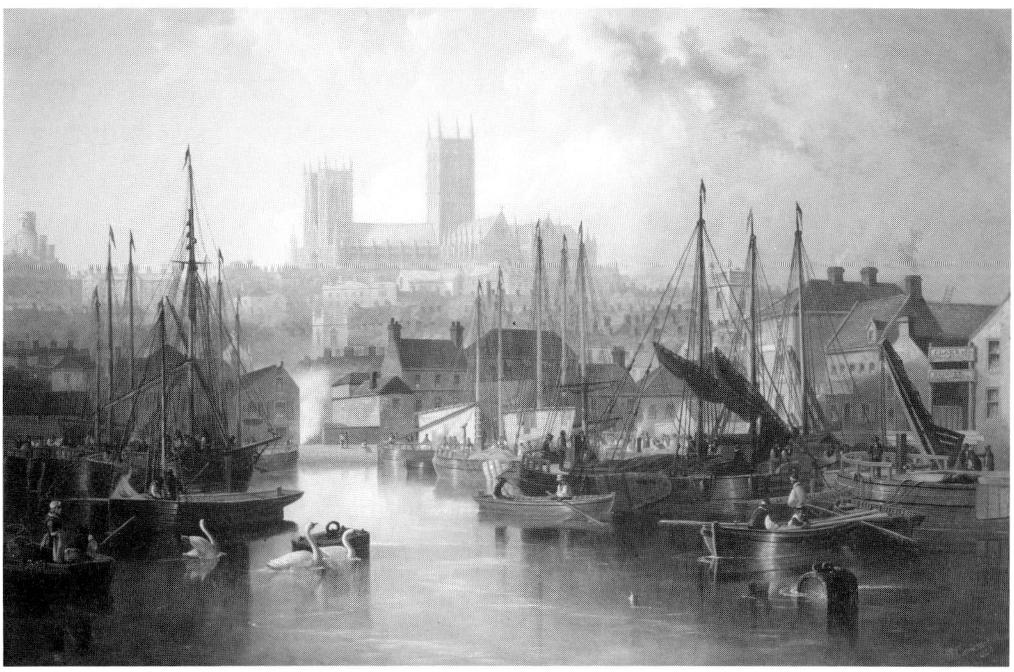

Brayford Pool and Lincoln Cathedral.
Lincolnshire County Council, Usher Gallery, Lincoln

appear from time to time in the sale rooms must be assumed to have been rushed work done for his 'bread and butter', for he was always mindful of his responsibilities towards his family and the quality of life he could afford to give them.

FAMILY LIFE

We hear little of how they fitted into the London life but Carmichael, when away, wrote regularly and there are references in his journal[32] to "his dear Wife, Happy Home and Children". However the attitude of his children clearly worried him when he refers to parents bringing their family through severe trials, strained anxiety and hard work both mentally and bodily. Thus winning a laurel for the family "which they might wear if they followed the same track, but they will not do it." He goes on to say ..... "the bones and directive means are all laid down, many times at the risk of life, for the steerage of our families, yet unhappily the children with all the good examples that have been taught them, do not follow up the Parent's course but bang away in the opposite direction."

By the summer of 1853 the Carmichaels had moved out of Howland Street to the cheaper district of Marylebone. The house is still there; in those days it was number 8 Milton Street (now 15 Balcombe Street) and it stands on the east side between Dorset Square and what in the 1850s was called the New Road, but was already being referred to as the Marylebone Road. According to a contemporary Ordnance Survey map, No. 8 Milton Street would have been part of a solid block of houses with small gardens, and there were mews buildings behind the Carmichael house. Their new home was smaller than their last but the top windows on the fourth floor look as if they would have let in sufficient light to be used as a studio. It was this address that Carmichael gave with his exhibit in the Royal Academy that year, 1853. It showed another northern scene *A Wreck and a Ruin – Tantallon Castle on the Firth of Forth*. *The Art Journal* gave him much praise "..... It is the best picture we have seen by this artist" they wrote and what pleasing words for Carmichael to read, in a year when his picture was hung two away from his rival Clarkson Stanfield (who was then showing his *HMS Victory with the body of Nelson on board*).

RUMBLES OF WAR

During 1853 the artists began to have other things on their minds for rumblings were coming from Eastern Europe where Russia was watching Turkey. In August there was a Review of the Royal Navy held at Spithead, and it drew the marine artists to Portsmouth. Carmichael did several pictures of this occasion; there are four sepia watercolours in the Royal Collection and he did two drawings that were engraved in the *Illustrated London News* Naval Review Supplement.[33]

The picture below shows the Queen, Prince Albert and two Princes (Prince of Wales and Prince Alfred) on their way in the Royal Barge to inspect the flagship, the *Duke of Wellington*. In the Royal Collection there is one of this scene that shows two boats of sailors in the forefront to the right of the picture; no doubt Carmichael would have had more time to spend on this than the one needed rapidly for engraving. The other in the *Illustrated London News* was entitled *The Engagement - Twenty Five minutes to Four*. As they described it "Suddenly that dark grey which enveloped the horizon changed colour, and white cloudy pillars took its place ..... crashing thunder filled the air. The battle had begun; the discharge of every broadside communicated an impulse to the

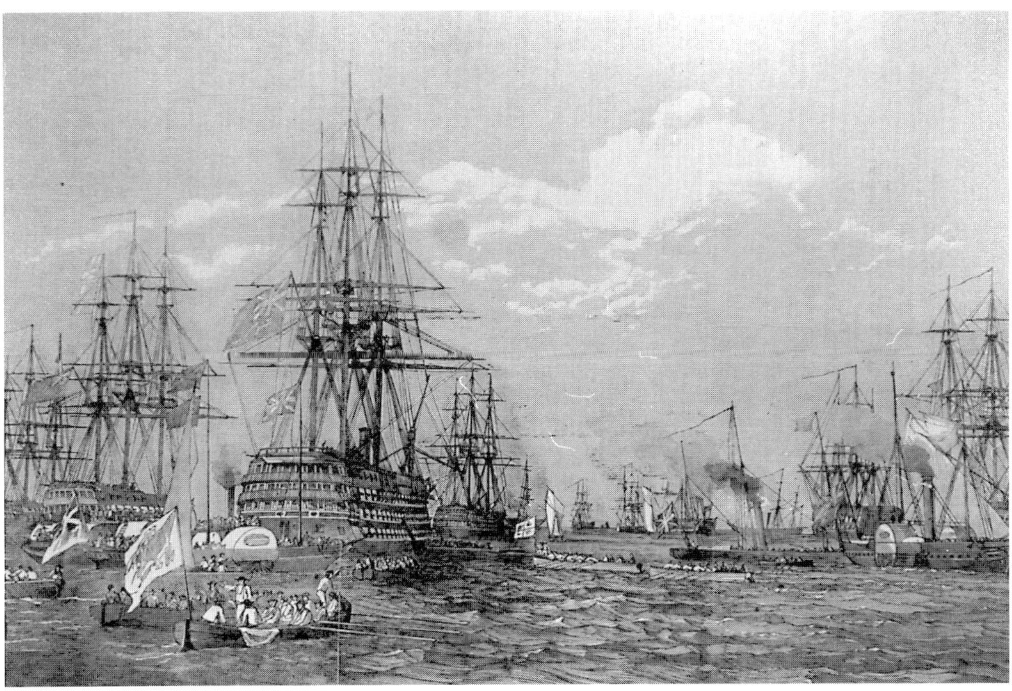

HM Queen Victoria proceeding to the flagship Duke of Wellington.
Illustrated London News Naval Review Supplement August 1853
Photographer Robin Crampton

atmosphere, which was felt as well as seen ..... and a feeling of deep thankfulness rose, as the thunder roared ..... that it was mimic and not real warfare to which we were listening ..... The engagement did not last many minutes and in its brevity it was probably a closer imitation of what a naval conflict will be, than if the firing had continued much longer".

However optimistic were these words, history has proved them wrong. Within twelve months there was full scale war and many of the marine artists, including Carmichael, started drawing very different pictures.

Eight

THE BALTIC

Many artists were needed to send enough pictures back to be engraved in the pictorial press of the day, of which by the mid 19th century there were many. These publications claimed that "Wherever there is any moving accident by flood or field, the `special artist' of the illustrated newspaper is found `taking notes' ..... the special artist may be said to have commenced his career with the Crimean War ..... and during the whole course of the war special artists were on the shores of the Black Sea and the Baltic".[1]

As we have seen in Chapter 6, it often took several artists to make up an engraving, so seldom is there only one particular artist's signature at the bottom of the final picture. Attached to the *Illustrated London News* for the whole or part of the Crimean War were the names of Joseph Arthur Crowe; William Simpson; Edward Angelo Goodall; Constantin Guys; Gustave Dore; Oswald Brierly; and Carmichael, who had had drawings previously accepted for engraving.[2]

LIFE AS A WAR ARTIST

He left London on board the *Countess of Lonsdale* on 26th May 1855, and was seen off at Gravesend by his seventeen year old son Ben, Annie who was four years older and her fiancée Mr. W.L. Thomas,[3] aged twenty five, himself an artist and engraver who also worked for the *Illustrated London News*. Carmichael sailed to Hamburg, took a train to Kiel and caught the mail packet to Copenhagen where he called on the British Ambassador. From there he travelled to Elsinore and, as he had time to wait, he paid a boatman the equivalent of £1 to row him a little way out to sea to make a sketch of the shore. He also called on the British Consul to collect some letters of introduction and left with him his sketches of Elsinore to be forwarded to London. He then boarded the ss *Royal Adelaide* that was loaded with provisions to be delivered to the Royal Navy. It was that same day, June 2nd 1855 that the following announcement appeared in the *Illustrated London News*.

> "We have the satisfaction to announce that on Saturday last, Mr. J.W. Carmichael, the celebrated marine painter, formerly of Newcastle upon Tyne, sailed for the Baltic, to sketch the Events of the War for the Illustrated London News. The

Sketches by this distinguished Artist, as they are received will be engraved in our Journal, so as to present a series of illustrations of the operations on the coming Campaign in the Baltic."

Two days later the *Royal Adelaide* met up with the frigate *HMS Cossack* who brought the news of the Massacre of Hango-Head. They told of how they had taken some fishermen prisoners but decided to release them "to show that it was not with wretched fishermen that England makes war". The boat returning them to the shore flew a white flag of truce and as the prisoners were landed about three hundred Russian brigands appeared and even though the leader could speak English, he ordered his men to massacre the British sailors and their prisoners. One man survived to tell the tale. Carmichael listened to this story and from the descriptions and his notes,[4] he drew the scene and this, the first engraving of his time as a war artist, appeared on the front cover of the *Illustrated London News* on 23rd June 1855.

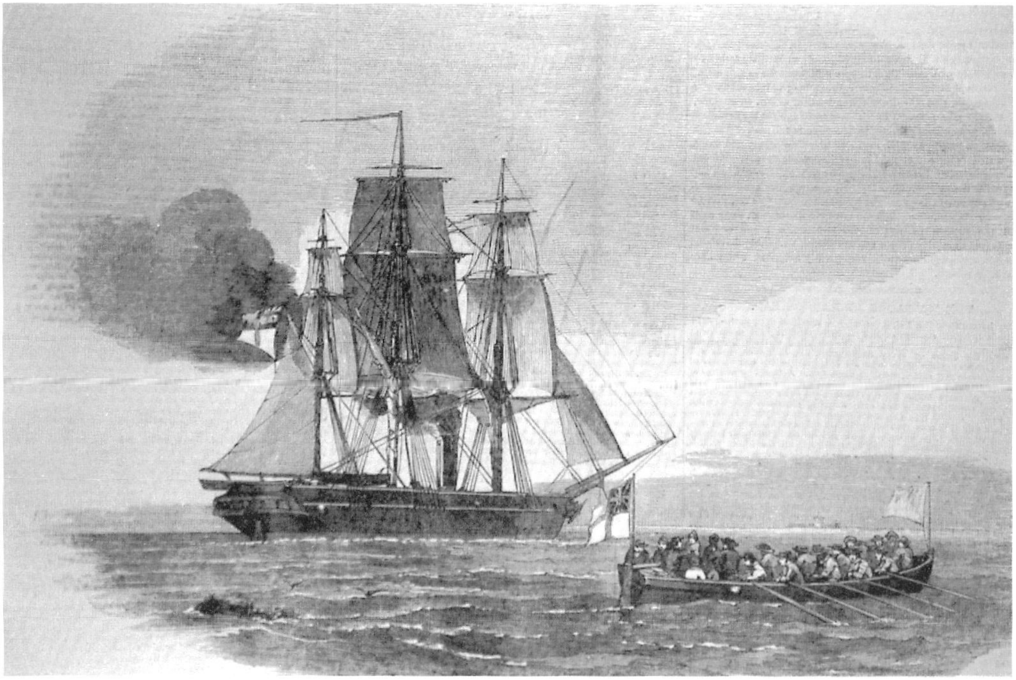

Massacre at Hango Head.
Illustrated London News 30th June 1855. Photographer Robin Crampton
This picture shows the prisoners being rowed ashore, flag of truce in full view.

By 8th June Carmichael had joined the gunboat *HMS Starling* and in spite of his accommodation, he did not complain of its position "..... where I sleep is within three yards of the powder magazine and the revolver pistols hang above your head under the deck with the sixty eight pounder above you .....". Soon they had joined the rest of the Fleet six miles off Cronstadt.

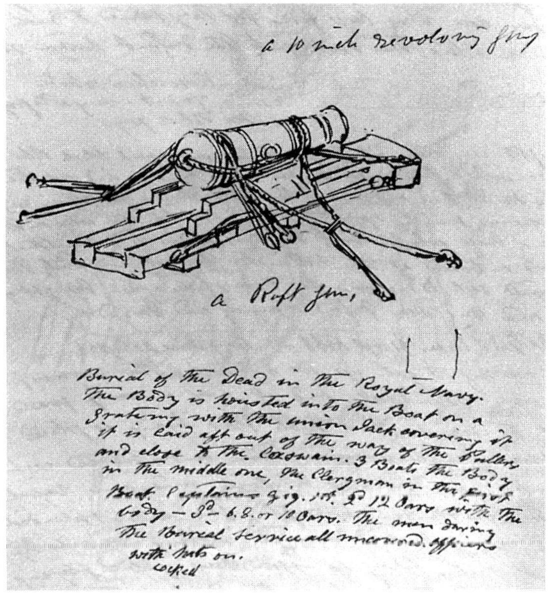

A page from his journal

A Raft Gun –
Notes on Burial at Sea

Private Collection
Photographer Robin Crampton

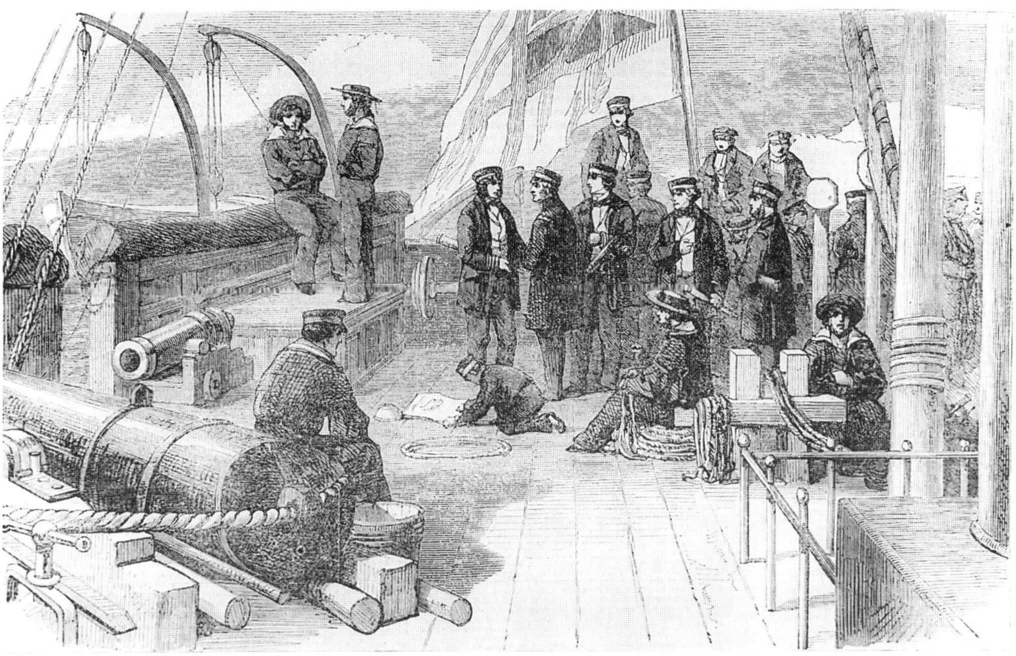

Quarter Deck of HMS Merlin. *Royal Naval Museum, Portsmouth*

French and English Officers taking a survey of Cronstadt, particularly the huge batteries of Risbark and "We clearly saw the spires of St. Petersburg glittering in the sun."

Frequent notes in his journal point to the fact that Carmichael's output of sketches sent back to London from the Baltic was vast. He had after long practice developed a rapid method of working and with a few strokes of his pencil could indicate a passing scene by a kind of pictorial shorthand which was afterwards translated and extended into the finished drawing. By 26th June thirty three sketches had been dispatched and by 31st July sixty five.

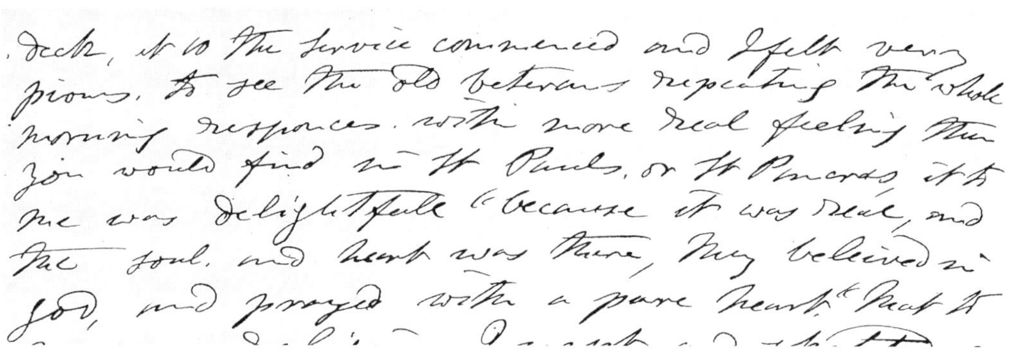
deck, at 10 the service commenced and I felt very
pious, to see the old veterans repeating the whole
morning responces. with more real feeling than
you would find in St Pauls, or St Pancras it to
me was delightfulle "because it was real, and
the soul, and heart was there, they believed in
God, and prayed with a pure heart"

Extract from Carmichael's journal at the time – ".... the service commenced and I felt very pious, to see the old Veterans repeating the whole morning responses with more real feeling than you would find in St Pauls, or St Pancras, it to me was delightful because it was real, and the soul, and heart was there, they believed in God, and prayed with a pure heart".

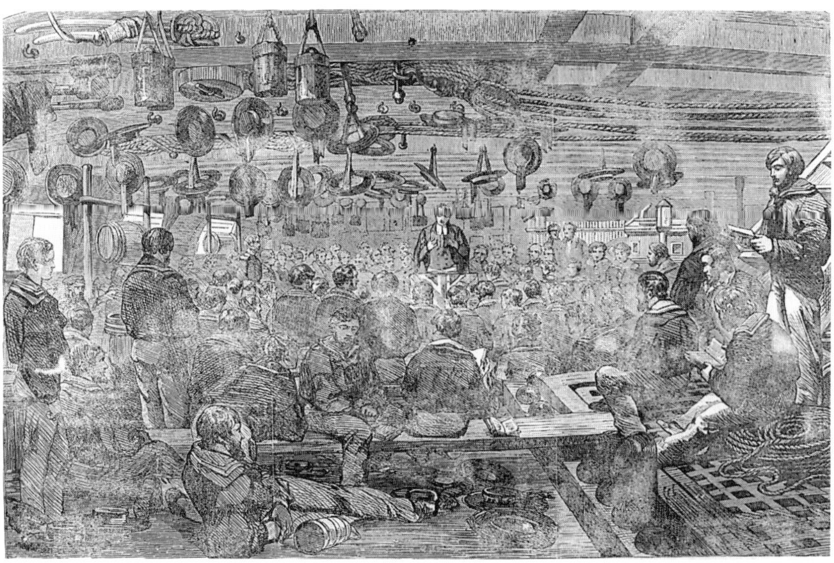

Final engraving of Divine Service on board the Caesar.
Illustrated London News 14th July 1855

On the 30th June again he made the front cover with the picture on the previous page of British and French officers on the quarter deck of *HMS Merlin* and, on the 14th July 1855, there was an engraving showing divine service on board *HMS Caesar.* Carmichael had sketched this four weeks earlier and the description that he wrote in his journal gives the reader an insight of a religious, caring and deep thinking man.

The 'family man' comes through with an entry on 12th July (his daughter Annie's wedding day) "I have been wondering all day how my dear little daughter Annie is and how she has undergone this day, to her certainly the most exciting in her life ..... she leaves her home, where there lives an incomparable Mother, loving Sisters and Brothers ..... however I know William, (William Thomas), and feel happy with him as a son-in-law and I know he will live happy with my Annie ."

But such sentiments were fleeting and Carmichael remained the whole time continually conscious that he was there as a war artist. One of his most interesting descriptions is of the Russian mines (the infernal machines) – the drawing here shows only slight alteration from the final engraving that appeared

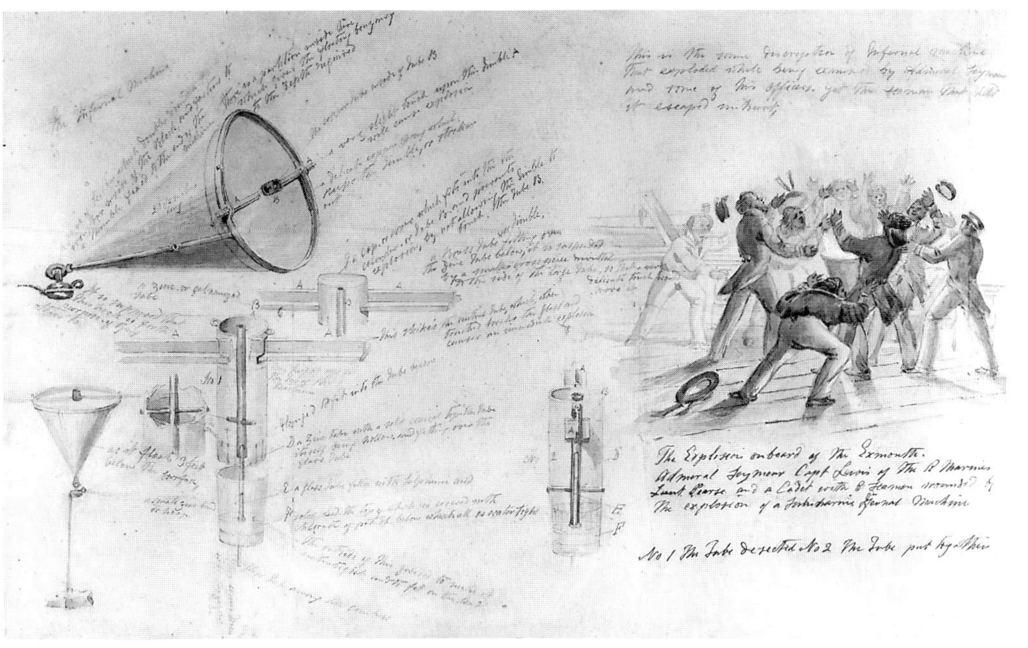

Explosion of a Russian Infernal Machine. *Pencil and Watercolour. Laing Art Gallery, Newcastle upon Tyne (Tyne and Wear Museum)*

in the *Illustrated London News* for July 21st 1855. It also includes a near disaster when one of the mines blew up on the deck of *HMS Exmouth* as it was being examined by the Admiral and some of his officers. Miraculously no-one lost their lives. Carmichael's descriptions show that he had a good technical grasp of how the infernal machines worked for his sketches are perfect in detail. He mentions that the explosive matter was not gunpowder but some combustible matter, and the artist in him adds "the smoke was too black in the sunlight to be gunpowder".

The highlight of his time in the Baltic was the bombardment of Sveaborg. The attack started on the 9th August and part of the time Carmichael watched from the deck of *HMS Edinburgh* making sketches throughout, together with notes for his future paintings "..... Sublime explosions ..... black silky masses of smoke filled with deep vermilion fifty times more bright but quite as red if not more so ....". And this is shown in one of the scenes he painted on his return to England *The Bombardment of Sveaborg* which is in the National Maritime Museum in Greenwich (see colour plates). Another view of the Bombardment also appeared as an engraving on the front cover of the *Illustrated London News* on September 8th 1855 and there was a further picture a week later that explained to the readers that the "..... sketch was taken when the fire was at its greatest height, which was about 3.0 p.m. on Friday 10th August, four weeks before the final bombardment of Sebastopol .....".[4]

Carmichael left the Baltic on the 14th August taking the chance to join a ship going to Dantsic. From there he travelled via Berlin, Potsdam and Cologne to Ostend, and so to Dover and London where his journal ends "..... reached home at half past five a.m. on the Monday morning the 20th August having left on the 26th May 1855 having been absent 12 weeks and 1 day." He must have contacted the *Illustrated London News* directly on his return for in the 25th August 1855 edition there is a piece that starts "The following graphic account of the Bombardment of Sveaborg is from the Artist who was present at the commencement."

That summer Carmichael's drawings were responsible for over 40 engravings and references to his work were still noticeable in 1856 when they published another memento of the Baltic in the 16th April issue – *A Pic-Nic in the Baltic*.

To celebrate the end of the Crimean War, there was a Fleet Review with 240 ships drawn up in two lines off Portsmouth. "The Review of such a fleet as the world never before beheld ..... covered a space of more than 12 miles ....."

reported the *Illustrated London News* on 26th April 1856, and two engravings of this appeared in the same issue, *The Fleet from the South* and a view he made of the ships from the deck of *HMS Blenheim*. He was also asked by several of the Captains who had been out in the Baltic to do pictures of their ships.

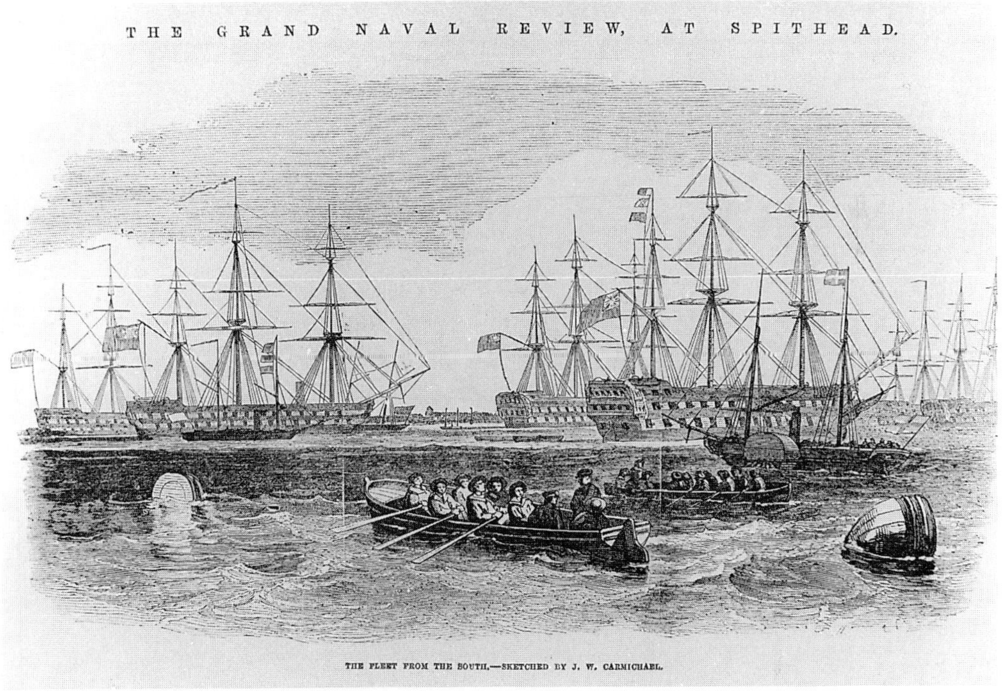

The Grand Naval Review at Spithead - The Fleet from the South.
Royal Naval Museum, Portsmouth

It was a busy time for Carmichael so it was not surprising that after a run of nine years he did not exhibit anything in the Royal Academy in 1856. But a year later he showed *Tantallon Castle and the Bass Rock - Firth of Forth*, and in 1858 he was back with a Baltic scene *The Entrance to Pillau in the Baltic*. This delicate, peaceful picture is a small composition for one of its size (20" x 32") and was highly commended in *The Art Journal* that year[5] when they wrote "This is a bright and clear picture and looks finished with long and patient labour. The water is painted with a truth that cannot be surpassed; the craft lie in the water under sail, with a heel and a movement which no other marine painter can give to his vessels; yet with all these qualities the picture is placed next to the ceiling. These are the crying injustices which must, in the end, bring about a great change in this institution."

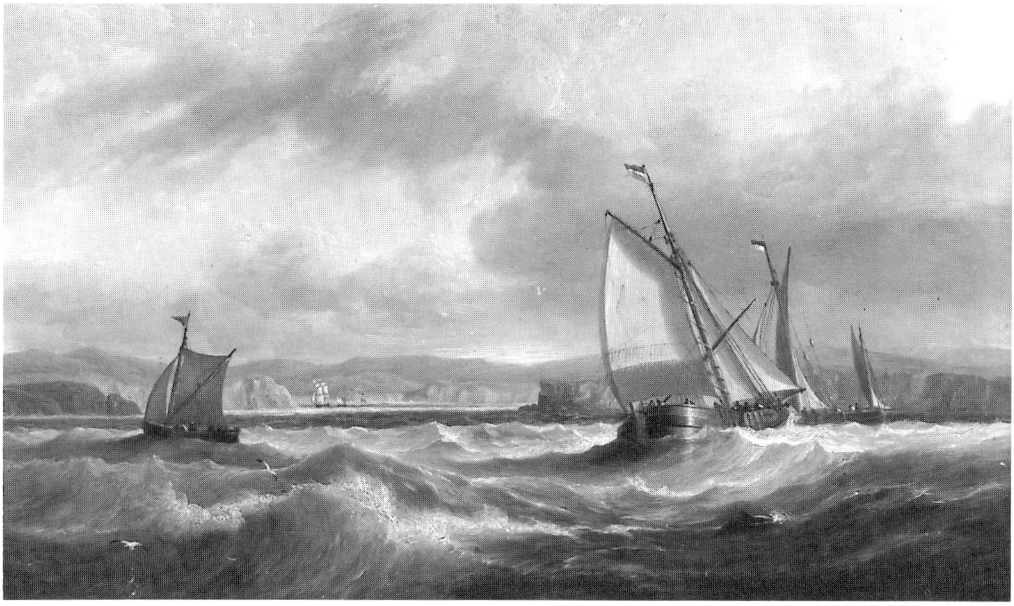

Hela near Dantzic - Baltic. *Christies Images, London.*
Carmichael continued for some years to turn his sketches from the Baltic into finished paintings. This was painted in 1860.

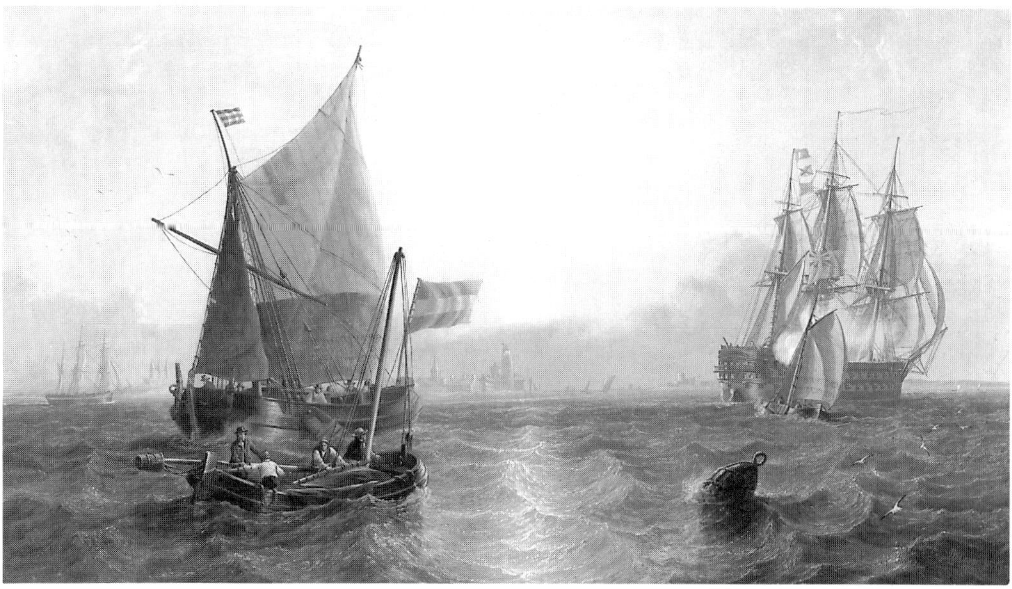

Entrance to Pillau in the Baltic. 1858. *Polak Fine Art Dealers, London.*
Carmichael exhibited this picture at the Royal Academy in 1858

As already mentioned Carmichael, like many other artists, was a great admirer of Turner and, in the journal he kept at the time he was a war artist, he mentions Turner's name more than once. So perhaps it was to escape from his war pictures, or maybe it was in his memory (Turner had died six years previously), that in 1857 Carmichael painted *A Recollection of Turner.* This was a smaller copy of what has become to be known as the *Bridgewater Piece* – a picture that the Duke of Bridgewater commissioned Turner to paint to match one of his Van de Velde pictures. Carmichael may never have seen the original though it was exhibited at the British Institution in 1857.

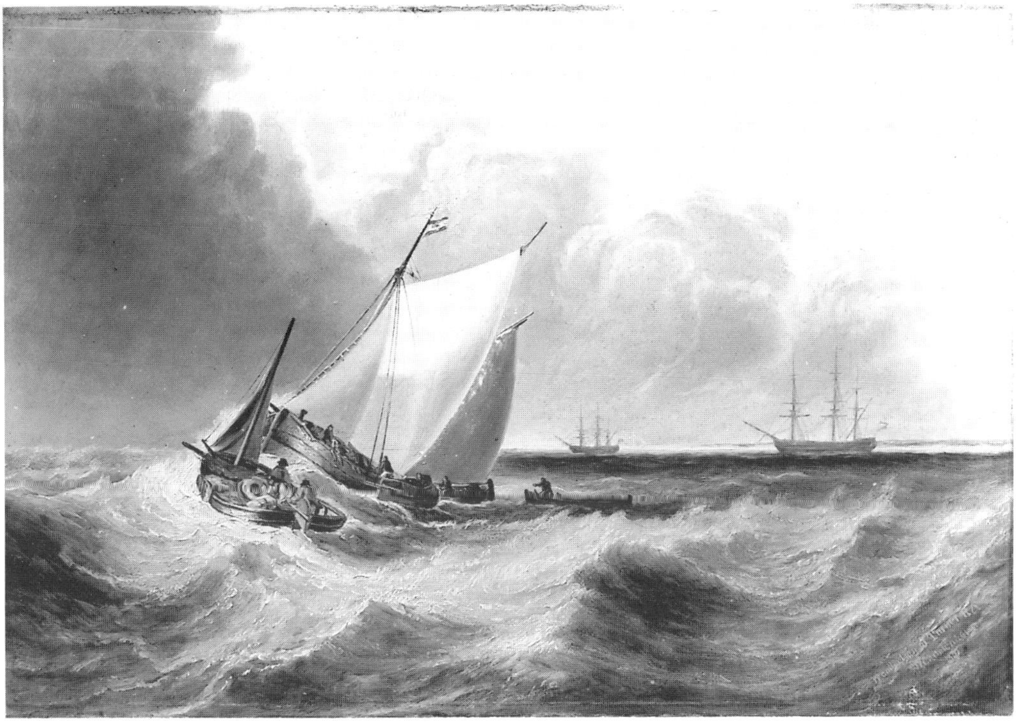

A Recollection of Turner.
Laing Art Gallery, Newcastle upon Tyne (Tyne and Wear Museum)

That year, the largest ship of the day, the *Great Eastern*, was being built at Millwall and in 1857 Carmichael painted two watercolours of her, one stern view and the other broadside. In this one he has once again shown his skill in making a ship portrait into a picture. The lines of the 680 feet hull are 'broken' with the activity of several fishing boats and of course the upright piece of wood and the seagull is there!

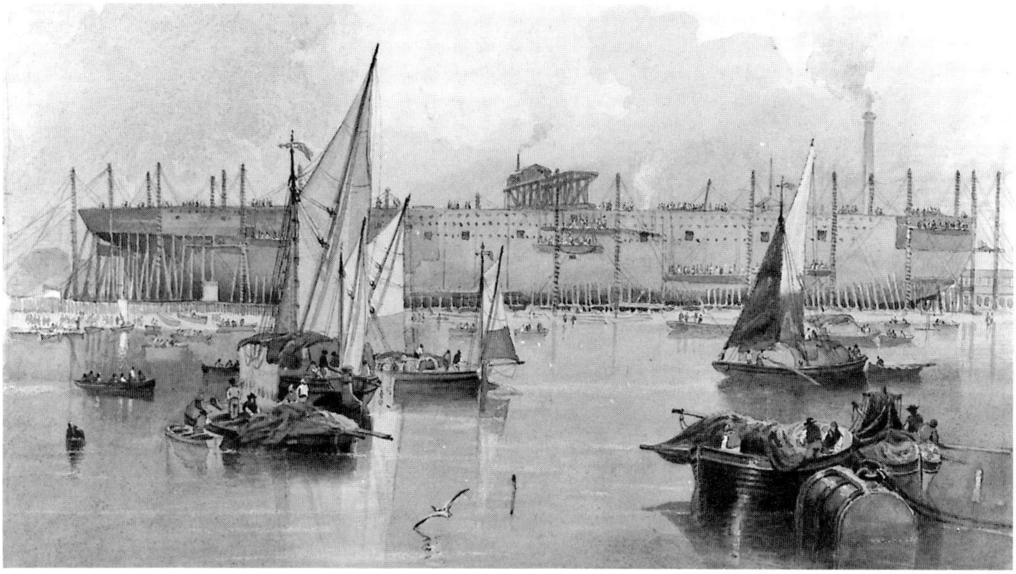

The Building of the Great Eastern 1857. *National Maritime Museum, London.* This was the third of Isambard Kingdom Brunel's great ships amd was painted by Carmichael for an engraving in the Illustrated London News.

We know that in 1857 Carmichael travelled to Italy and Switzerland because he did a painting of *Lake Maggiore* and another of *Lausanne* from sketches he signed 'on the spot'. In the late 1850s he did several pictures of views in the north of the country *Off Tynemouth*, *Robin Hood's Bay, Yorkshire*, a *View of Durham* and others.

If the late 1850s were busy painting years, they were also busy domestically. Their second daughter Polly was married in July 1856 to a Newcastle shipowner, Henry Scott, at the Marylebone Parish church (still in the Marylebone Road). Also John and Mary became grandparents again when their elder daughter Margaret bore a second son, Herbert (who was to become Herbert Schmalz the artist), and their daughter Annie had her first child, William. Annie went on to give birth to a daughter in 1858 and another son, Frederick, in 1859.

Sometime after the summer of 1859 the Carmichaels moved from Milton Street to the north of Regent's Park and east of Primrose Hill, which in those days would have been country. Whatever the reasons for the move, the family no doubt enjoyed the position of their new home, 13 St. Mark's Crescent, and the 1861 census showed that only they lived there. The house still remains, one of a neat curved street of houses on the edge of the Regent's Park canal. On its bank stands St. Mark's church which was newly built when the Carmichaels arrived. We know this move would have been after the 1859 Royal Academy exhibition as Carmichael gave the Milton Street address for his two exhibits that year.

The move may also have been for health reasons. Aaron Watson mentions in his memoir of Carmichael in those years of how he wrote of "incessant work and some domestic trouble". There is no indication that his marriage was anything but happy so the domestic trouble was more than likely the health of his son Jack; as far back as 1855 Carmichael's journal refers to "poor Jack".

His 1859 exhibits were to be his last at the Royal Academy and one of these was his favourite coastal town *Scarborough from the North Bank Top – Morning*. However once again it was 'skied' and while the reviewers admired such "an effective picture" and the way it had been "worked up to an extremely careful finish", they again criticised the authorities when they said "if such qualities do not entitle works to be placed so that they can be seen, the conclusion is, that after certain pictures are placed, merit has but little claim to consideration." Carmichael's other exhibit that year *Start Light – Coast off Devonshire* was not even mentioned. This would have been somewhat disheartening, but he exhibited two more paintings at the British Institution, in 1861 and 1862, when *A Scene in Holland* was well received "..... the boats are drawn, rigged and floated in a manner that has never been accomplished in any other similar works that have ever come under our notice ....." said *The Art Journal*.[6] For his painting at the British Institution in 1862 Carmichael went back to another Scarborough view *Scarborough Morning* and sold this work for seventy guineas.

FIRST BOOK WRITTEN

In 1859 Carmichael was commissioned by Winsor and Newton to write a small handbook on the subject of marine painting. This surely was an indication that his work as an artist was respected for there were other artists who could have been approached; Edward Duncan,[7] for instance had illustrated three titles in

Vere Foster's series of practical painting books and, back in 1826, the Royal marine painter, J.T. Serres,[8] had published a handbook for marine painters, but there was obviously a demand for another.

Carmichael approached this assignment most humbly "The writer of this little treatise" he says "..... is fully sensible of the difficulties of his position as an author, and does not presume to arbitrarily lay down rules of Art .....". *The Art of Marine Painting in Water-colours* is a small handbook, barely 8" high, and was written for the student. Costing 1/-, it sold well and later, in 1862, Winsor and Newton asked Carmichael to write the companion to it *The Art of Marine painting in Oil Colours*.

On the 1st November that year at the age of thirty two, their son Jack died of consumption and they buried him in Finchley Cemetery. According to all records Jack's death had a profound effect on both his parents. Carmichael was then sixty three and his wife Mary five years younger. Perhaps it was this tragedy, or a feeling that London had little more to offer, or the fact that his friend Carrick had moved there to study photography, that made them choose Scarborough.

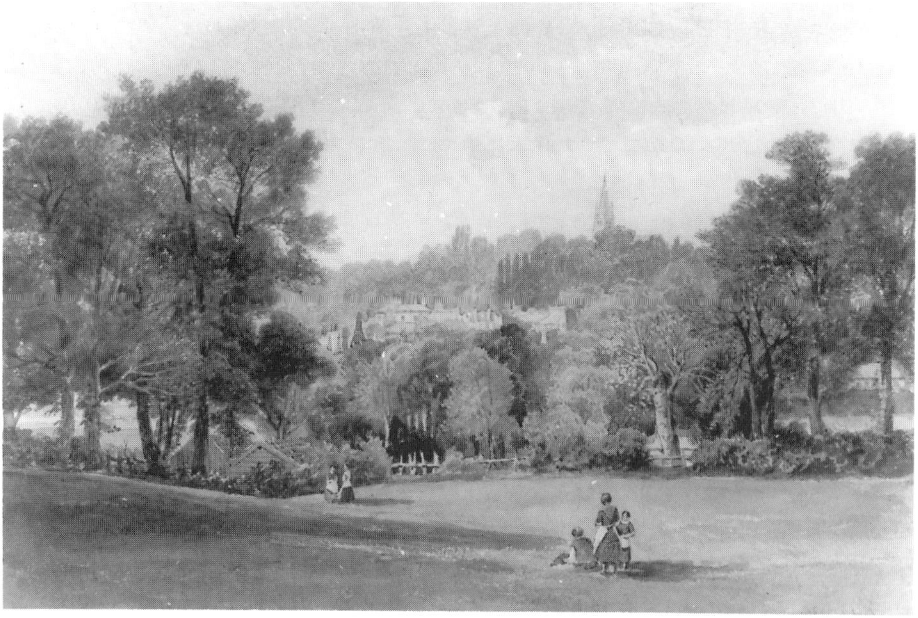

On Hampstead Heath. 1863. *Sotheby's, London*
Carmichael sketched this scene before leaving London and completed the painting in 1863, the year the family arrived in Scarborough.

Nine

SCARBOROUGH THE LATER YEARS

Apart from the sentimental attachment that Carmichael had for this north eastern resort, Scarborough was a good place to choose for his final home. Since 1626 when the Spa Wells had been discovered, the potential of the town had been there, but like Brighton in the south of the country, it had taken the British public's interest in sea bathing and their healths for the authorities to realise the future of Scarborough as a health resort. By 1863 when the Carmichaels arrived there, the population of 13,000 had turned their simple 'medicinal well' into a thriving business and earned their town the name of 'Queen of the Watering Places'.

Scarborough was not just a holiday resort. For years it had been the only safe harbour for coastal traders plying between the Tyne and the Humber rivers. With the plentiful supplies of oak timber from the North Riding, her shipbuilders had built many large colliers to cope with the Northumberland coal boom. Then over the horizon was to come the development of iron shipbuilding, and it meant that Scarborough's harbour and shipyards were no longer capable of dealing with the increase in the size of the vessels. The last big ship was built there in 1863, the year the Carmichaels took up residence.

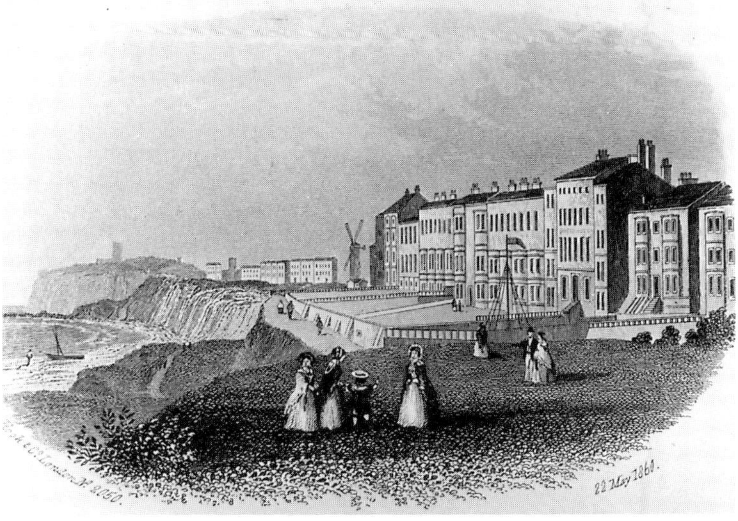

This picture from a contemporary engraving shows North Cliff. No. 18 Mulgrave Terrace is one of the buildings on the extreme left of the cliff top next to the Castle.
Marshall Hall. Newcastle upon Tyne

They found lodgings at the top of a four storey Victorian house, 18 Mulgrave Terrace. The house is still there (the houses are now numbered as part of Castle Road). It was a bright terrace that had only been completed just before the Carmichaels arrived when the expansion of the town had demanded more accommodation for visitors. The narrow ridge on which it had been decided to build a selection of lodging houses was steeped in history. On the one side there was a wide sweep of the North Bay and up to the ancient Castle, and from the other side of the house could be seen the 12th century church of St. Mary's, behind which the old Church Stairs lead steeply to the harbour and South Bay. No artist could have asked for better surroundings or to live with a better view.

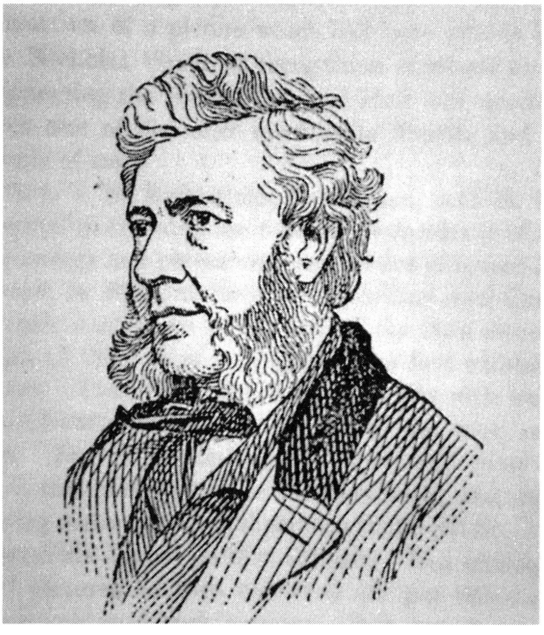

John Wilson Carmichael.
Newcastle upon Tyne Central Library.
Photographer Robin Crampton

This is the last picture that we have of Carmichael; he still has a good head of hair and he has broadened. It is difficult to tell from what is little more than a sketch but perhaps the eyes now have a sad look, the twinkle has gone from them, but the determination is still there.

SECOND BOOK WRITTEN

He moved to Scarborough with much unfinished work and many plans. One of his first projects was to finish his second book the *Art of Marine Painting in Oil Colours*[1] and he planned this in a different format to the first. This time his idea was to show the building up of a picture by using letters – perhaps the first painting by numbers? First he drew a pen and ink outline of, say, 'River craft'. Then he would break this down into letters arranged alphabetically and the student would have his example to follow. For instance, at the letter 'H', the instructions

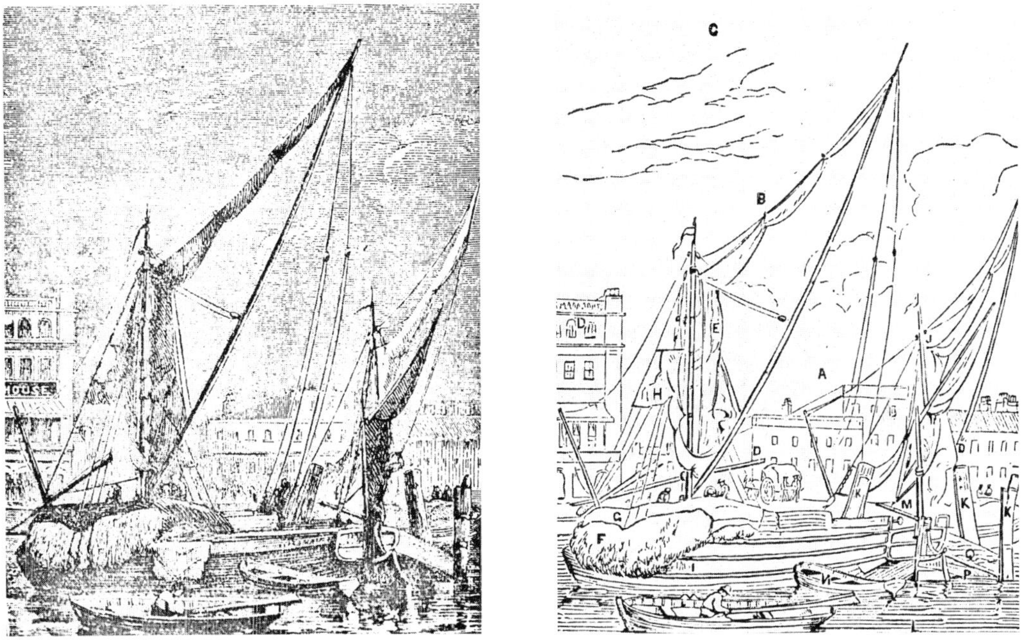

The Art of Marine Painting in Oils. *by J.W. Carmichael.*
Photographer Robin Crampton

were to paint the foresail with the same colours as 'E' with the addition of a little brown ochre. Then at the letter 'I', the hull must be laid in with bitumen, mummy, madder brown and lamp black. 'J' for the distant sail, madder, brown ochre and lamp black. And so on through outlines showing cloudy and tranquil skies, cliff subjects, and stormy seas to the detailed painting of other craft.

Carmichael must have found it a long and laborious task, occupying time that he would no doubt have preferred to have spent creating his own pictures. However early in 1865 the finished work brought flowery praise from *The Art Journal* "Indeed nothing is omitted that can render the book perfect in itself; the plain instructions require only application on the part of the student to render him independent of any other assistance .....". This book, like the other sold well, but at 1/- a copy it would not have reaped great financial rewards.

Neither the money nor the words of praise for this small publication would have helped the family through their next tragedy – the death of their second son Benjamin who died suddenly from acute pneumonia in November 1864 almost two years to the day of the death of his brother, and the family travelled to London to bury him next to Jack in the Finchley Cemetery.[2]

CARMICHAEL'S HIGH OUTPUT OF WORK

In spite of everything Carmichael managed to carry on working, though the strain on him showed in one of his journal entries around that time when he talks of working hard "..... amidst great anxiety and discouragement, but always with the same gratitude to God and unwearied patience." But his old determination was still there and, perhaps to publicise his book, and certainly to silence any of his critics who might have thought he had 'retired' in Scarborough, he painted one of the finest pictures of his career, a large oil of *Sunderland Harbour*. He probably did this from sketches as he has painted in the old tide light that had been removed in 1856. (see colour plates).

He did several views of Sunderland in the 1860s and other paintings showing his detailed shipping in different backgrounds. Perhaps they were pictures that brought back memories of more active days or of places that he had never visited and wished he had, such as *Moro Castle – Cuba* which was based on some sketches by Captain Hotham RN[3] and *Two Naval Deckers and other shipping off Cape Town*. He also completed a large oil painting of *Dunstanburgh Castle.*

There was some unfinished work or ideas that he had brought with him from London. Among these *Calshot Castle* and *Off Herne Bay*, and then, in

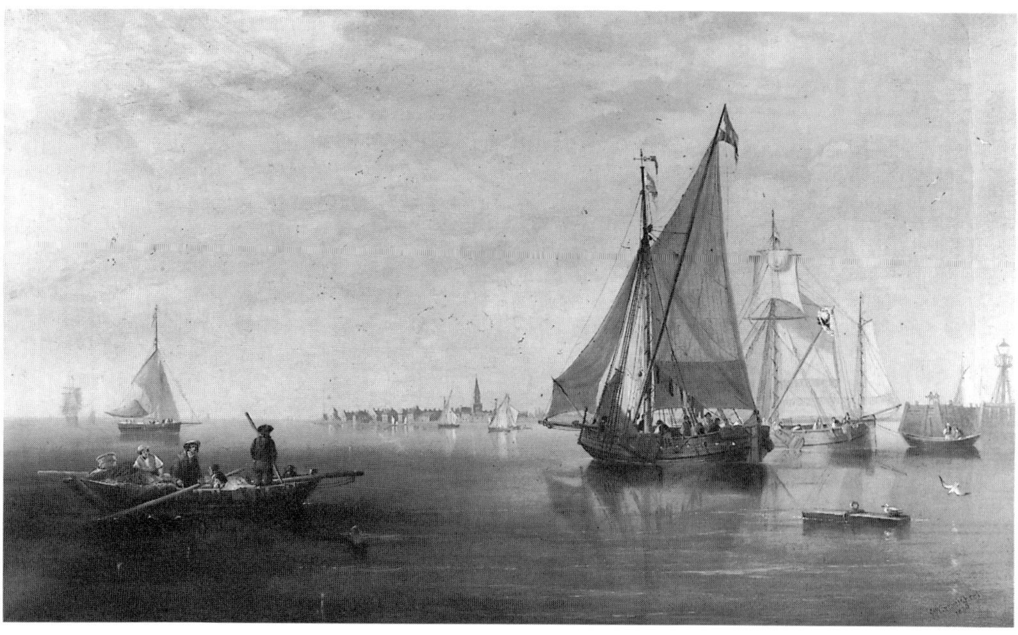

Fishing Vessels in a Calm off Port Texel. 1865. *Christies Images, London*

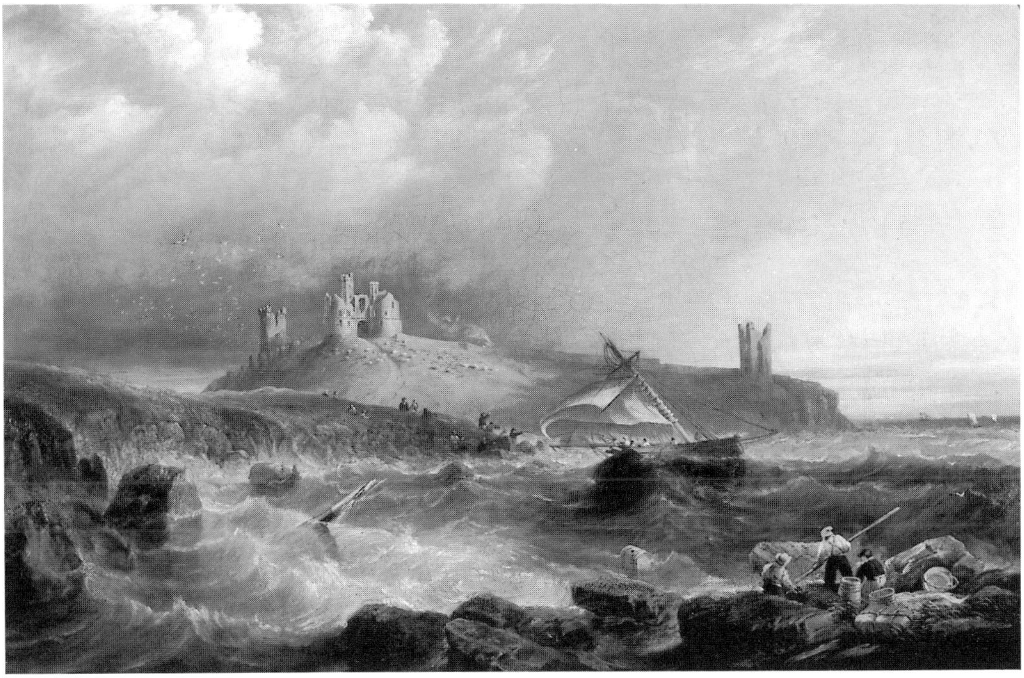

Dunstanburgh Castle. 1865. *The Lord Mayor of Newcastle upon Tyne*
This large oil, which hangs in the Manion House, was painted three years before Carmichael died and shows he retained his skill with both composition and colour. (Note the similarity in composition with another view of Dunstanburgh Castle in Chapter 7 done eighteen years earlier).

what must have been one of the last commissions he received from his patron the 3rd Earl of Bolton, he painted two pictures: one of *Broadstairs – Kent*, and the other of *Margate – Kent.*

Scarborough was developing fast and the now famous Grand Hotel was starting to be built to offer elegant accommodation for the wealthy, and they like the not so rich holidaymaker were eager to take home with them pictures of their holiday venues. Carmichael was quick to notice this, and many of his works in those last years were smaller pieces featuring the northern holiday resorts or beauty spots. When he died he was working on a large series of about 40 sepia views of scenes on the North East coast from Yorkshire to Berwick on Tweed which were evidently intended for engraving.

Of course at the time there were other artists painting for the holidaymaker too. Atkinson Grimshaw[4] was painting his poetic effects of the sea and harbour

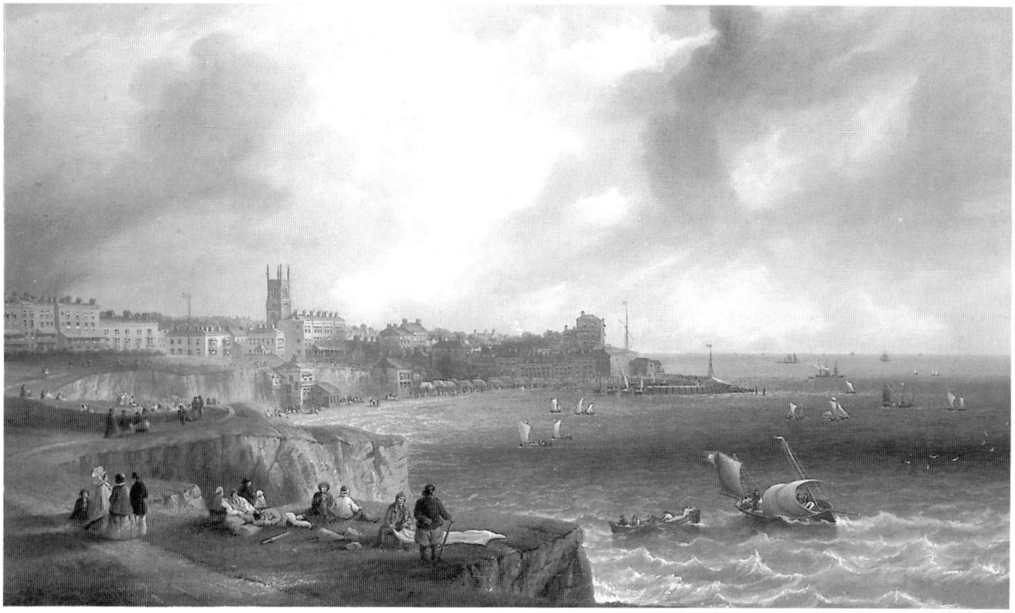

View of Broadstairs. 1863. *Polak Fine Art Dealers, London*

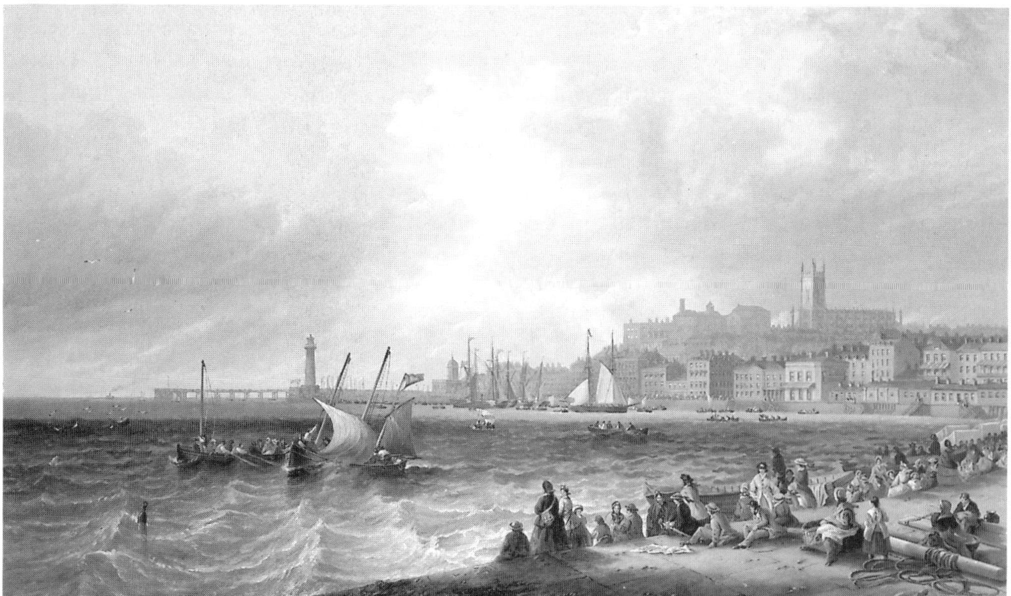

View of Margate. 1863. *Polak Fine Art Dealers, London*

in moonlight; Henry Redmore[5] had a picturesque record of shipping in the Humber and Whitby, Scarborough and Flamborough Head, often done from the sea; and H.B.Carter[6] was also painting coastal scenes of Scarborough. But it is probably true to say that Carmichael was the first nationally known artist to paint so many pictures of the town. It was a good time for the artists for soon the newly developing photography would take over much of the tourist market.

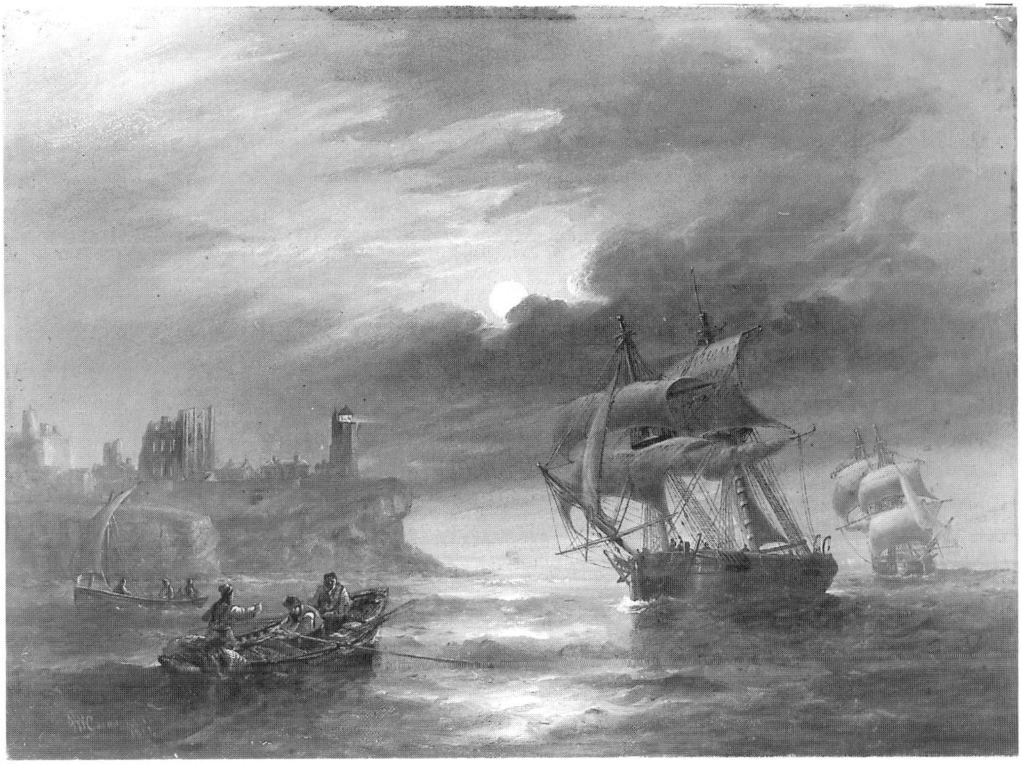

Shipping off Scarborough. *Sotheby's, London*
This moonlight scene painted in 1864 shows a vague resemblance to Atkinson Grimshaw

In spite of the tragedies that the family had suffered in recent years, Carmichael would have got much enjoyment from painting his local surroundings, some of which might have reminded him of his early days on the Quayside in Newcastle. Even though there were no longer any big ships being built in Scarborough, there were still small boatbuilders building their fishing yawls and cobles and there was a busy harbour for an artist to watch and draw. Scarborough Borough Council have several fine pictures that Carmichael left behind, but no works of his have been definitely attributed to 1868, the year he died. However this rough watercolour sketch, only 4" x 14", a view of *Scarborough Castle from Scalby*, was probably one of his last.

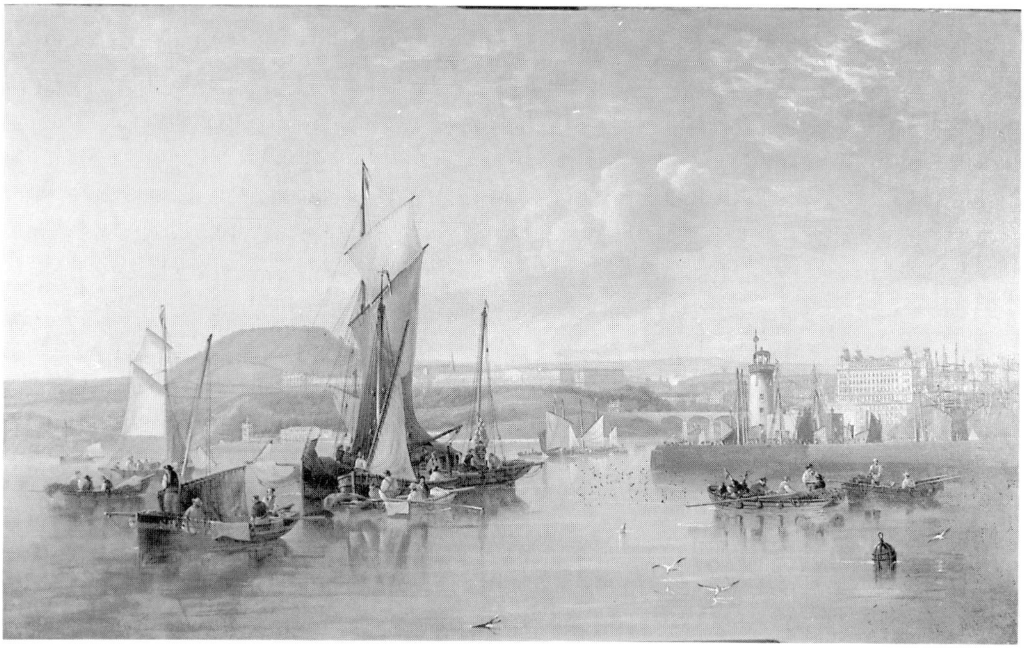

Scarborough from the sea. 1867. *Scarborough Art Gallery*
Carmichael painted this impressive oil the year before he died.

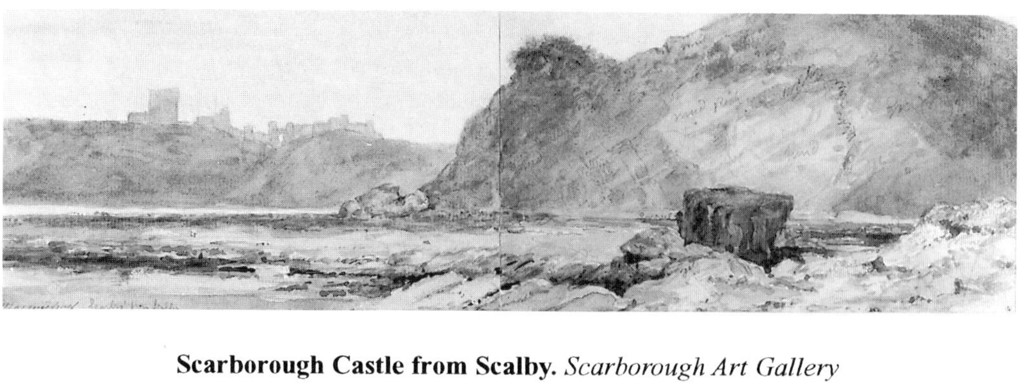

Scarborough Castle from Scalby. *Scarborough Art Gallery*

John Wilson Carmichael died on 2nd May 1868, aged sixty-nine. The death certificate states that he died at his home and under 'cause of death' is written "Epileptic Seizure, Apoplexy certified." Two days later they carried his coffin from Mulgrave Terrace across the road to St. Mary's church for the funeral service.[7] It was a strange day to choose because the 4th May was his wife Mary's sixty-fourth birthday. He was buried in the Dean Road cemetery in Scarborough; the records say that this took place the following day, the 5th May.[8] On the grave stone is written "He was beloved and esteemed by all who knew him."

He left a simple Will – "Effects under £1,000, the will of John Wilson Carmichael formerly of the Borough and County of Newcastle-upon-Tyne but late of Scarborough in the County of York, Artist deceased who died 2nd May 1868 at Scarborough aforesaid widow the relict the Sole Executrix."

Carmichael's obituary in *The Art Journal*[9] ran to half a column. They wrote of him being "..... Gifted with an eye of rare accuracy and a hand ready in the delineation of form ....." and went on to say that no other painter had studied marine art with so much enthusiasm and success and of how he "..... had produced at the very entrance of his career works which brought his name prominently before the public ..... and with respect to coast-scenery it may be said that he has painted almost every remarkable feature between the Thames and the Firth of Forth." Slight exaggeration but then this perhaps is permitted in an obituary, and John Wilson Carmichael with his sense of humour would certainly have enjoyed reading it.

Ten

CONCLUSION

However profusive were the words of Carmichael's obituary in *The Art Journal*, several of the facts they mention are inaccurate and vague indicating that they knew little about him or his career. It probably sums up Carmichael in his lifetime that, while he was popular amongst his own small circle, he was not widely known; certainly he was not fully appreciated; and probably if we did but know, he died feeling that he had not 'quite made it'. For instance he never became an RA and, in spite of being twice 'skied' with his work at the Royal Academy, he never became a member of the Royal Society of Painters in Water-Colours which was founded in 1804 by several artists who felt that their work was not properly shown at the Academy.

Carmichael always wanted to do as well as another northern artist, Clarkson Stanfield,[1] but he remained in his shadow and Stanfield became a full member of the Royal Academy in 1835. We have proof of Carmichael's feelings of envy from William Bell Scott's anecdotes when he talks about Carmichael's plans to leave Newcastle for London ..... "nothing would stop him. He would leave the provinces cut out Stanfield, and make his fortune great and name immortal."[2]

As Watson says in his memoir "It is questionable whether Carmichael strengthened his art by his removal to London" and a number of critics would agree with this. His work shows little development during his time there and compared with his contemporaries he exhibited few pictures; 21 at the Royal Academy, 21 at the British Institution, and 6 at the Society of British Artists. Whereas his friend Thomas Carrick exhibited 144 pictures at the Academy and his rival Clarkson Stanfield 135. But Carmichael certainly painted a large number of pictures, and this is apparent in a sale catalogue of the Thomas Sopwith collection[3] held in September 1879 where out of 396 paintings, drawings and sketches, 196 were Carmichael's. And then there was the sale of his work two years after his death[4] when over 1,000 sketches and 90 watercolour drawings were sold and only fetched £174.15.0d. How sad it is that he is not here today to see the kind of prices that his work is now fetching.

Carmichael's prolifacy worked for and against him. In the provinces it was the secret of his success as William Bell Scott[5] writes in his anecdotes "The secret of his manner of life has been that his little sea-pieces were so popular he habitually made a good deal of money in the course of the year. Dealers used to take his small pictures, a dozen at a time, to the universities and elsewhere, and at this time boating-men had a tendency to indulge their taste in pictures as well as boats, so that they competed for 'Carmichaels'. One morning I went into his studio and found eight or ten small pictures fixed up before the fire to facilitate their drying. Looking from one to another of these and finding them essentially all the same – representing mid-day, a fresh sea, blue openings of sky amidst breezy white and grey clouds, a yacht, and a fishing-boat tacking or going before the wind to the right or left – I suggested that he might indulge in a change now and then, and so give us morning or sunset, storm or dead calm. His answer at the time posed me considerably, but it was a wise one, showing the sound mind in a sound body. He affirmed that no one would buy the kind of art I described for art's sake; that ordinary people would only buy what they saw and enjoyed every day, or wanted to enjoy: the fresh sea, mid-day with a blue streak to the sky."

However in London he would have found it more difficult to find this sort of buyer for his pictures and, as David Cordingly says (in his *Marine Painting in England 1700-1900)*[6] "His weakness was a lack of originality and a too obvious wish to please his clients." But surely that is what Carmichael was pointing out to Bell Scott when he talked of what type of art the ordinary person wished to buy? Now, some 150 years later, such sea-pieces are way beyond the means of the people Carmichael had in mind.

Another criticism came from C.E. Hughes[7] when he talks of Carmichael's compositions being "... very unequal in merit. Many of them are full of dignity and a fine understanding of the motion of water and the animation of shipping, but others are dull and uninteresting." Perhaps he is right for critics do talk of Carmichael being repetitive with his compositions, but this can be explained by him painting too many pictures too quickly.

Some people would agree with Aaron Watson when he queries whether Carmichael was wise to ever leave Newcastle where he was both well known and living among people who knew of his upbringing and accepted him for his art. By moving to London he immediately put himself under pressure; he was still a respected artist but we have no evidence that he became involved in any of the many intellectual sets. Perhaps he was too humble, or perhaps he did not wish to spare the time, so he remained on the periphery.

Everyone would agree with Denys Brook-Hart[8] that Carmichael "had a considerable ability for draughtsmanship, so that his vessels look just right on whichever point of the wind they happen to be sailing." And A.H.H. Archibald[9] is right when he says of him that "as an artist he belongs to the circle of Clarkson

Stanfield and Edward Cooke[10] and at his best is the equal of Stanfield." And indeed Carmichael and Stanfield's work have been confused.

Carmichael contributed to 19th century painting an intimate knowledge of ships, thus ensuring a high degree of accuracy that can be relied upon as a record of our ships at a time when steam was beginning to take over from sail. With his ship portraits he was to the 19th century what Samuel Scott[11] was to the 18th and both artists had to wait for a long time to be fully appreciated. Oliver Warner[12] goes so far as to say that, for a successor to Carmichael's technical study of craft, we have had to await the work of Borlase Smart.[13]

Carmichael has at last achieved a name for his marine art, having been in his own lifetime a good, but not a great, artist. But he was certainly an attractive one who could be relied upon for applying the strictest detail, and he was typical of the period in which he lived.

While he has gone down in history as a marine artist, it would certainly be remiss to close his story without mentioning his many landscapes. After all, as a young man when he first met Thomas Miles Richardson,[14] he came under the influence of a northern artist who became nationally famous for his Northumberland scenery. If you look at Carmichael's oil painting of *Westoe Village* completed in 1838 (see colour plates), the only sign of water the artist has allowed himself is a small glimpse of a stream in the foreground.

While his family background, his environment and his personal interests led him to become foremost a marine artist, his landscapes also show amazing skill. Perhaps it is fitting to end this book with two fine examples of his painting, one painted from the shore and the other from the sea. Surely these are the work of an artist who most would agree has, with the passing of time, proved himself to be – great?

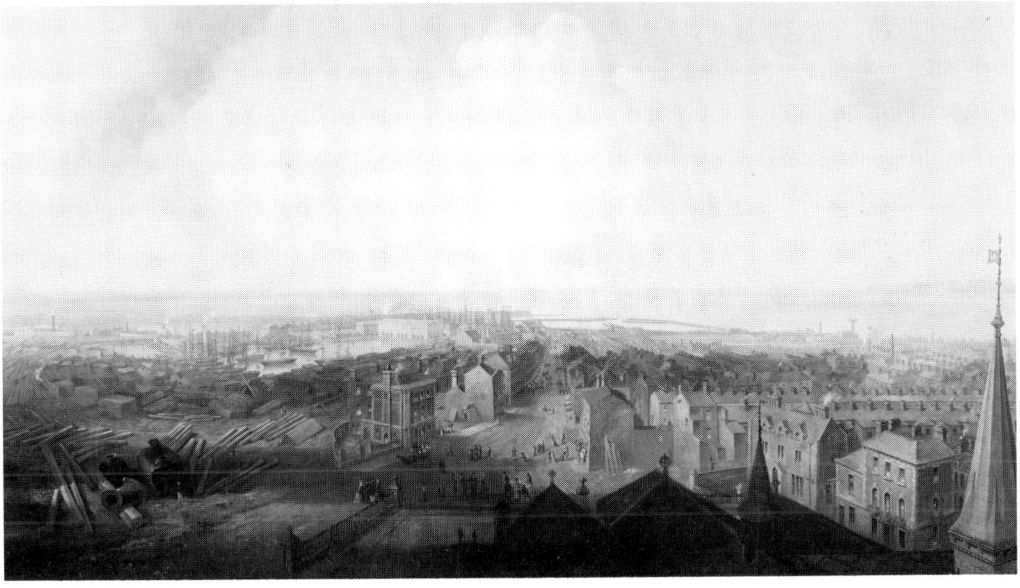

West Hartlepool from the Tower of Christ Church. 1858.
Hartlepool Museum Service

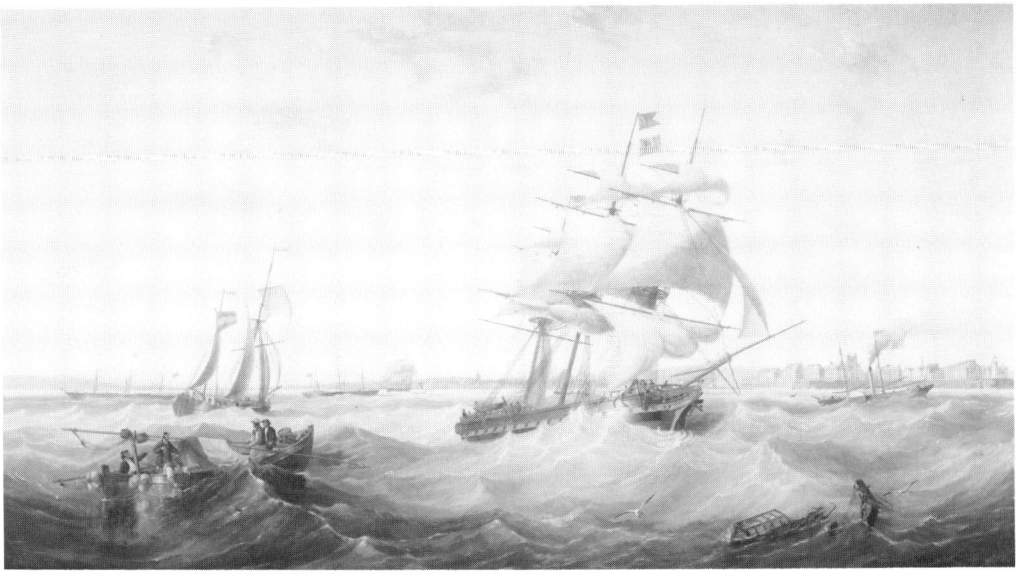

West Hartlepool from the Sea. 1856. *Hartlepool Museum Service*

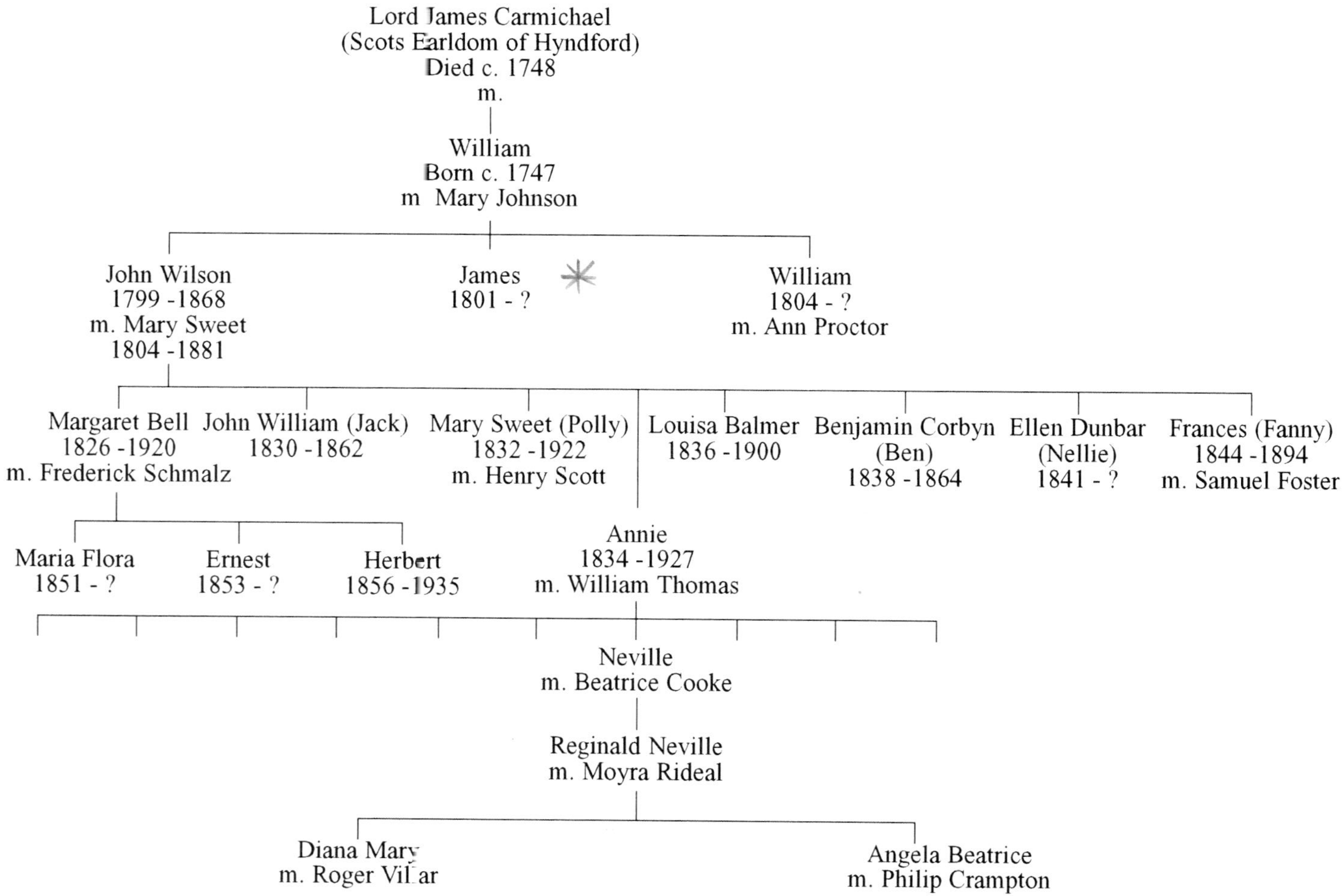

* See 'The Fine and Decorative Art Collections of Britain and Ireland' p. 187 (Ironbridge Gorge Museum Trust)

Eleven

JOHN CARMICHAEL'S FAMILY

After his death Mary Carmichael left Scarborough and went back to Newcastle to live at 48 Waverley Terrace in Elswick, a residential part of the city. In the 1871 census she describes herself as "Widow" and her occupation as "Assistant"; also with her was one of her unmarried daughters, Ellen, who was then aged 30 and gave her occupation as "Daily Governess". A local directory for 1880 shows that Mary had moved to Grove Street in Elswick and her other unmarried daughter Louisa, then aged 44, was nearby at 95 Westmoreland Road in a building described as a 'Seminary'.

Mary outlived her husband by thirteen years and, when she died in 1881, she was buried in Elswick cemetery. Louisa remained unmarried and probably returned to Scarborough for she died there in 1900 and was buried in the Dean cemetery with her father. Her sister Polly Scott was with her when she died, and put her own address as Albury in Sussex on the death certificate. Annie, the third Carmichael daughter, outlived her husband William Thomas by twenty-seven years. They had ten children and she died in London in 1927. Frances (Fanny) married Samuel Foster and they went to live in Runcorn in Cheshire. She died in 1894 and is buried with her mother in Elswick cemetery.

The eldest daughter Margaret Schmalz continued to live in Ryton. She and Frederick certainly had three children. Their second son Herbert[1] became an artist but, with the anti-German feelings during the First World War, he took his mother's maiden name of Carmichael, as did his elder brother Ernest who went into the Church, and their sister Flora.

Both Margaret and her brother Jack took seriously the idea that they were descended from Lord Carmichael (as mentioned in the Introduction) and, among family letters, there is one from Carmichael's granddaughter Flora, unfortunately undated, where she writes "Someone has said that Uncle Jack believed himself to be the rightful Earl of Hyndford and I know that some of my mother's friends used to call her Lady Margaret Carmichael".

BIBLIOGRAPHY

Armstrong, Richard – *Grace Darling - Maid and Myth.* Pub. Dent. 1965

Smedley, Constance – *Grace Darling and her Times.* Pub. Hurst & Blackett Ltd. London. 1932.

Middlebrook, S. – *Newcastle upon Tyne, its Growth & Achievement.* Pub. Kemsley House, Newcastle upon Tyne 1950.

Newcastle and Carlisle Railway with drawings by John Wilson Carmichael. 1st Pub. 1836. 2nd Pub. Frank Graham. Newcastle upon Tyne. 1969.

MacIntyre and Bathe – *The Man of War.* Pub. Methuen. 1968.

Metcalfe, Priscilla – *Victorian London.* Pub. Cassell. 1972.

Tallis, John – *Street Views with simple Maps of London.* 1839.

Bell Scott, William – *Autobiographical Notes and Notices of his Artistic and Poetic Circle of Friends.* Vol. 1. Pub. Osgood & McIlvaine. London. 1920.

Welford, Richard – *Men of Mark twixt Tyne and Tweed.* Vols. 1, 2, 3. Pub. Walter Scott Ltd., Paternoster Square, London. 1895.

Lofts, Norah – *Domestic Life in England.* Pub. Corgi. 1976.

Hughes, C.E. – *Early English Water-Colour.* Pub. Ernest Benn Ltd. London 1950. (First published in 1913).

Maas, Jeremy – *Victorian Painters.* Pub. Barrie & Rockcliffe. 1969.

Frere-Cook and Macksey – *The Guinness History of Sea-Warfare.* Pub. Guinness Superlatives. 1975.

Hall, Marshall – *The Artists of Northumbria.* Pub. Titus Wilson Ltd. Kendal. 1982.

Bradshaw's *Monthly Railway and Steam/Navigation Guide for 1846.*

Hardie, Martin – *Water-Colour Painting in Britain.* (Victorian Period) Ed. J. Mayne & B. Taylor. Pub. Batsford 1968.

Nicholl, John – *The Pre-Raphaelites.* Pub. Studio Vista. 1970.

Blakemore, Trevor – *The Art of Herbert Schmalz.* George Allen & Co., 44/45 Rathbone Place, London. 1911.

Rowntree, Arthur – *History of Scarborough.* Pub. Dent. 1931.

Gaunt, William – *Marine Painting.* Pub. Martin Secker & Warburg Ltd. 1975.

The Victorian History of the Counties of England. Vol. 2. The Borough of Scarborough. Yorkshire North Riding.

Lindsay, Jack – *Turner. The Man and his Art.* Pub. Granada. 1985. Pub. Mackays of Chatham Ltd.

Richardson, Benjamin Ward – *Thomas Sopwith - Excerpts from his Diary.* Pub. Longmans. 1891.

Jackson, Mason – *The Pictorial Press - Its' Origins and Progress.* Pub. Hurst & Blackett. London. 1885.

Berryman, Bryan – *Scarborough as it was.* Pub. Hendon Publishing Co. Hendon Mill. Nelson. 1977.

Edwards, Mervyn – *Scarborough 966-1966.* Pub. Scarborough Archaeological Society. 1966.

Brettell, Thomas – *Handbook to the Isle of Wight.* Pub. J. Mitchell. 3rd Ed. 1844.

Archibald, E.H.H. – *Dictionary of Sea Painters.* Pub. Antique Collectors Club. 1980.
Fisher, W. Stanley – *A Dictionary of Watercolour Painters. 1750-1900* Pub. W. Foulsham & Co. London. 1972.
Wood, Christopher. *Dictionary of Victorian Painters.* Pub. Antique Collectors' Club. 2nd Edition. 1978.
Cordingly, David – *Marine Painting in England. 1700-1900* Pub. Studio Vista. 1974.
Whitley, William – *Art in England 1821-1837.* Pub. Cambridge University Press. 1930.
Lamb, G.F. – *Franklin, Happy Voyager.* (Being the Life and Death of Sir John Franklin.) Pub. Ernest Benn Ltd. London. 1956.
Graves, Algernon – *The Royal Academy of Arts, Complete Dictionary of Contributors and their work from 1769-1904.* Pub Kingsmead. 1905.
Graves, Algernon – *The British Institution – 1806-1867.* Complete Dictionary of Contributors and their work from its foundation. Pub. Kingsmead. Bath. 1875.
Johnson, Jane – *The Royal Society of British Artists. 1824-1893.* Works exhibited. Vol. 1. Pub. Antique Collectors' Club 1975.
Pictures of Tyneside. Reproductions of engravings from drawings by J.W. Carmichael. Edited by Middlebrook. Pub. Oriel Press Limited. Newcastle. 1969.
Mackenzie, E. – *History of Newcastle upon Tyne.* Pub. Mackenzie & Dent, Newcastle. 1827. (2 Vols bound in one). Brook-Hart, Denys – *British 19th Century Marine Painting.* Pub. Antique Collector's Club. 1974.
Warner, Oliver – *British Marine Painting.* Pub. Batsford Ltd. London. 1948.
Millar, Delia – *Queen Victoria's Life in the Scottish Highlands.* Pub. Philip Wilson Ltd., Covent Garden. 1985.

CATALOGUES, BOOKLETS AND ARTICLES

Carmichael Centenary Exhibition, Laing Art Gallery. 1968. Catalogue prepared by Miss Nerys Johnson.
The Missing Years at Scarborough by Marshall Hall. *Arts and Antiques.* October 15th. 1977.
Catalogue for *Painters of the Sea* exhibition. Brighton Art Gallery and Museum. 1979. Prepared by David Cordingly.
Catalogue for *The Art of the Van de Veldes* held National Maritime Museum, 1982. Prepared by David Cordingly and Westby Percival-Prescott.
Catalogue *Art for Newcastle.* Newcastle Festival 1984. Prepared by Paul Usherwood and Kenneth Bowden. Exhibition at Laing Art Gallery.
Catalogue *John Wilson Carmichael* exhibition for Newcastle Festival 1982 by Tyne and Wear County Council Museums. Prepared by Andrew Greg.
Memoir by Aaron Watson, appears in *Picture of Tyneside* with descriptive letter press by Richard Welford, published in Newcastle in 1881.
Graham, Frank – *Newcastle.* Pub. Frank Graham. 1978.
The Graphic Jubilee Number. 20th June. 1887.
The Art Journal.
Sailing Sketches by John Wilson Carmichael. Laing Art Gallery, Newcastle. 1986.

REFERENCES

Chapter 1

1. Also mentioned in *The Art of Herbert Schmalz* (Carmichael's grandson) by Trevor Blakemore. Pub G. Allen & Co. 1911.
2. Memoir by Aaron Watson that appears in *Pictures of Tyneside* with descriptive letter press by Richard Welford. Pub in Newcastle in 1881. Pub Oriel Press, Newcastle. 1969.
3. *Newcastle upon Tyne* by S. Middlebrook. Pub S.R. Publisher Ltd., Yorkshire. 1968.
4. *History of Newcastle upon Tyne* by E. Mackenzie. Pub Dent. 1827.

Chapter 2

1. Memoir by AaronWatson that appears in *Picture of Tyneside* with descriptive letter press by Richard Welford. Pub in Newcastle in 1881. Pub Oriel Press, Newcastle. 1969.
2. *History of Newcastle upon Tyne* by E. Mackenzie. Pub Dent. 1827.
3. Henry Perlee Parker. 1795-1873.
4. *Newcastle upon Tyne* by S. Middlebrook. Pub S.R. Publisher Ltd., Yorkshire. 1968.
5. Edward Swinburne. 1765-1847.
6. Thomas Bewick. 1753-1828.
7. Joseph Crawhall. 1793-1853.
8. John Dobson. 1787-1865.
9. James Ramsay. 1786-1854.
10. John Wykham Archer. 1806-1864.
11. Robert Mackreth. 1766-c.1860.
12. George Gibsone. 1762-1846.
13. Thomas Good. 1789-1872.
14. John Martin. 1789-1854.
15. George Balmer. 1805-1846.
16. John Ewbank. 1799-1847.
17. Edwin Henry Landseer. 1802-1873.
18. B.R. Haydon. 1786-1846.
19. John Varley. 1778-1842.
20. John Frederick Lewis. 1805-1876.
21. A. Callcott. 1779-1844.
22. George Chambers. 1803-1840.
23. Clarkson Stanfield. 1793-1867.

Chapter 2 (Continued)

24. Francis Danby. 1793-1861.
25. J.B. Chrome. 1794-1842.
26. John Ward. 1798-1849.
27. David Cox. 1738-1859.
28. J.T. Serres. 1759-1825.
29. Joseph Mallord Turner. 1775-1851.
30. Both paintings are in the British Museum.
31. Part of a sale of the Thomas Sopwith collection held on 16th and 17th September 1879 at The Academy of Arts, Blackett Street, Newcastle upon Tyne.

Chapter 3

1. John Martin. 1789-1854.
2. John Scott. 1802-1885.
3. Thomas Thorpe. 1812-c.1855.
4. *Newcastle upon Tyne* by E. Mackenzie. Pub Dent. 1827.
5. John Dobson. 1787-1865.
6. In a journal that Carmichael kept during his assignment to the Baltic for the *Illustrated London News*. Private Collection.
7. From the Library of J.R. Abbey. In the Elton Collection, Ironbridge Gorge Museum Trust, Telford, Shropshire.

Chapter 4

1. Memoir by Aaron Watson. Published Newcastle in 1881. Pub again in *Pictures of Tyneside* by Oriel Press, Newcastle. 1969.
2. Willem van de Velde. 1610-1693. His son Willem 1633-1707.
3. Joshua Reynolds. 1723-1792.
4. Joseph Mallord Turner. 1775-1851.
5. Turner was looking at Van de Velde's *A Rising Gale* after which he painted a companion to it *Dutch Boats in a Gale.*
6. E.W. Cooke. 1811-1880.
7. *Marine Painting 1700-1900.* Pub Studio Vista, London. 1974.
8. A. Canalletto. 1697-1768.
9. Thomas Girton. 1775-1802.
10. Salvator Ross. 1615-1673.
11. Titian. 1477-1576.

Chapter 4 (Continued)

12. In 1881 the pictures were published again by the Lambert family business under the title *Pictures of Tyneside or Life and Scenery on the River Tyne Sixty Years ago.* This edition contained 33 engravings from Carmichael's drawings. It was published again as *Pictures of Tyneside* by Oriel Press, Newcastle. 1969.
13. William Collard. 1792-1847.
14. Mark Lambert. 1781-1855.
15. Pub by T&J Hodgson, Newcastle. 1829 (P. 52)
16. *Art in England 1821-1837* by William Whitley. Pub Cambridge University Press. 1930. (P. 305)

Chapter 5

1. Both published by Winsor & Newton, London. *Water-Colours* in 1859 and *Oil Colours* in 1865.
2. Christies. November 24/25 1870.
3. Catalogue prepared by Andrew Greg, now curator of the Shipley Art Gallery, Gateshead.
4. Thomas Girton. 1775-1802.
5. Joseph Mallord Turner. 1775-1851.
6. In Private Collection. 4th June and 24th July 1855.
7. *Early English Water-Colours* by C.E. Hughes. Pub Ernest Benn, London. 1950. (P.139)

Chapter 6

1. Pub Ernest Benn Ltd, London. 1950. (P.20)
2. Thomas Henry Hair. 1810-1882.
3. Memoir by Aaron Watson that appears in *Pictures of Tyneside* with descriptive letter press by Richard Welford. Published in Newcastle. 1881. Pub Oriel Press, Newcastle. 1969.
4. Thomas Sopwith. 1803-1879.
5. Morpeth Hall Salerooms. Auctioneers Thomas Waters. 16th July 1947.
6. Nicholas Pocock. 1740-1821.
7. Thomas Carrick. 1802-1874.
8. *The Art of Marine Painting in Water-Colours* by J.W. Carmichael. Pub Winsor & Newton, London. 1859.
9. Clarkson Stanfield. 1793-1867.
10. E.W. Cooke. 1811-1880.
11. Robert Watson. 1815-1885.
12. John Reay. 1817-1902.

Chapter 6 (Continued)

13. Henry Perlee Parker. 1795-1873.
14. Robinson Elliott. 1814-1894.
15. David Dunbar. ?-1866.
16. Edward Hastings. 1781-1861.
17. George Harrison. 1816-1846.
18. Albany Hancock. 1806-1873.
19. *Grace Darling and her Times* by Constance Smedley. Pub Hurst & Blackett. 1932. (P.125)
20. Both letters in the Laing Art Gallery, Newcastle.
21. William Bell Scott. *Autobiographical Notes and Notices of his Artistic and Poetic Circle of Friends. Volume 1.* Pub Osgood & McIlvaine, London. 1920. (P.210)
22. *Grace Darling and her Times* by Constance Smedley. Pub Hurst & Blackett. 1932. (P.128)
23. Thomas Ellerby. c.1821-1857.
24. Journal in Private Collection
25. Catalogue in Northumberland Record office. 309/H1/25.
26. In the Elton Collection. The Ironbridge Gorge Museum, Telford, Shropshire.
27. Published in London. 1885. (Pp. 317 & 320)
28. Ebenezer Landells. 1808-1860.
29. Pub Philip Wilson, London. 1985.
30. In National Maritime Museum, London.
31. *Art in England 1821-1837* by William Whiteley. Pub Cambridge University Press. 1930 (P.2)
32. John Martin. 1789-1854.

33 & 34. *Autobiographical Notes of the Life of William Bell Scott and Notices of his Artistic and Poetic Circle of Friends. 1830-1882.* Ed. Minto. Pub James Osgood and McIlvaine. 1920 (Pp. 209 & 211)

35. Joseph Crawhall (the Second). 1821-1896.
36. David Cox. 1733-1859.
37. J.B. Chrome. 1794-1842.
38. John Varley. 1778-1842.
39. Thomas Miles Richardson (Senior). 1784-1848.
40. George Balmer. 1805-1846.
41. Bradshaw's *Monthly Railway and Steam Navigation Guide.* March, 1846.
42. Charles Brooking. 1723-1759.
43. William Van de Velde. 1610-1693. William Van de Velde (the son). 1633-1707.

Chapter 7

1. *Street Views with Simple Maps of London* by John Tallis. 1839.
2. John Constable. 1766-1837.
3. George Chambers. 1803-1840.
4. Thomas Carrick. 1802-1874.
5. Richardson (Junior) also called Thomas Miles. 1813-1890.
6. Henry Perlee Parker. 1795-1873.

7, 8, 9, & 10. From memoir by Aaron Watson that appears in *Pictures of Tyneside* with descriptive letter press by Richard Welford. Pub Newcastle in 1881. Pub Oriel Press, Newcastle. 1969.

11. *The Graphic* Jubilee Number. 20th June 1847.
12. *Autobiographical notes of the Life of William Bell Scott and Notices of his Artistic and Poetic Circle of Friends. 1830-1882.* Ed. Minto. Pub James Osgood and McIlvaine. 1920 (P.185)
13. Letter from Department of Art History, University of Auckland. 28th March, 1983.
14. *Franklin - Happy Voyager* by G.F. Lamb. Pub Ernest Benn Ltd., London. 1956 (P.260)
15. George Balmer. 1805-1846.
16. Joseph Mallord Turner. 1775-1851.
17. Thomas Butterworth. 1768-1842.
18. Nicholas Pocock. 1740-1821.
19. Samuel Drummond. 1765-1844.
20. Clarkson Stanfield. 1793-1867.
21. *The Art Journal*. 1st June 1848. (Pp. 170-171)
22. *The Art of Herbert Schmalz* by Trevor Blakemore. Pub G. Allen and Co. 1911. (P.14)
23. Memoir by Aaron Watson that appears in *Pictures of Tyneside* with descriptive letter press by Richard Welford. Pub Newcastle in 1881. Pub Oriel Press, Newcastle. 1969.
24. Anthony Copley Feilding. 1787-1855.
25. John Joy. 1806-1866. William. 1803-1867.
26. Henry Luscombe. 1820?-1868.
27. *Early English Water-Colours* by C.E. Hughes. Pub Ernest Benn, Ltd., London. 1950. (P.131)
28. Samuel Walters. 1811-1882.
29. William Huggins. 1781-1845.
30. Thomas Whitcombe. c.1752-1827.
31. *The Art Journal*. 1st June 1854. (P.158)
32. Journal in Private Collection.
33. *Illustrated London News* – Naval Review Supplement. August 1853. (Pp. 148 & 156).

Chapter 8

1. *The Pictorial Press - Its Origin and Progress* by Mason Jackson. Pub Hurst & Blackett, London. 1885. (Pp. 328-330). Also *The Artist as a Reporter* by Paul Hogath. Pub Gordon Fraser. 1986.
2. 20th August 1853. (P.148) *Grand Review of the Fleet at Spithead.*

   14th March 1855. (P.364) *The Baltic Fleet at anchor prior to going to the Baltic.*

   21st April 1855. (P.376) *The Pelican steamship approaching Dover to embark the Emperor Napoleon and the Empress.*
3. William Thomas. 1830-1900.
4. 7th June 1855. Journal in Private Collection.
5. *The Art Journal.* 1st June 1858. (P.166)
6. *The Art Journal.* 1st March 1861. (P.71)
7. Edward Duncan. 1803-1882.
8. J.T. Serres. 1759-1825.

Chapter 9

1. J.W. Carmichael. Pub Winsor & Newton, London. 1864.
2. St. Pancras High Road Cemetery, East Finchley, London, N2. Grave 31T.
3. Later became Admiral Sir William Hotham KCB
4. Atkinson Grimshaw. 1836-1893.
5. Henry Rudmore. 1820-1887.
6. H.B. Carter. ?-1867.
7. Recorded in Burial register of St. Mary's Church, Scarborough. 4th May 1868.
8. Grave Space C9-26.
9. *The Art Journal.* 1st July 1868. (P.128)

Chapter 10

1. Clarkson Stanfield. 1793-1867.
2. *Autobiographical Notes on the Life of William Bell Scott and Notices of His Artistic and Poetic Circle of Friends. 1836-1882.* Ed. Minto. Pub Osgood & McIlvaine. 1920.
3. Northumberland Records Office 309/H1/25. Vol. 1 (P.209)
4. Christies. 24th and 25th November 1870.
5. *Autobiographical Notes* Vol. 1. P.210 (as above)
6. *Marine Painting in England. 1700-1900.* Pub Studio Vista, London. 1974. (P.161).
7. *Early English Water-Colours.* Pub Ernest Benn Ltd., 1950. (P.131)

8. *British 19th Century Marine Painting.* Antique Collector's Club. Pub Baron Publishing. 1981. (P.40)

9. *Dictionary of Sea-Painters.* Antique Collector's Club. 1980 (P.79)

10. Edward Cooke. 1811-1880.

11. Samuel Scott. 1702-1772.

12. *British Marine Painting.* Pub Batsford, London. 1948. (P.34).

13. Borlase Smart. 1881-1947.

14. Thomas Miles Richardson (Senior). 1784-1848.

Chapter 11

1. Herbert Schmalz. 1856-1935. Exhibited 46 paintings at the Royal Academy.